D0766690

WebPlus X7
User Guide

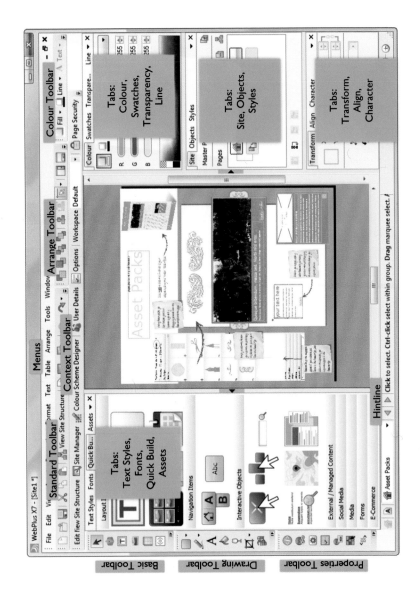

Contents

Contents

Welcome

Welcome!

Welcome to WebPlus X7 from **Serif**—the easiest way to get your business, club, organization, personal interest, or household on the web!

To make life so much easier, WebPlus offers you a simple way to build websites visually, without having to learn or use any traditional web programming. WebPlus comes with an impressive selection of **design templates**, page **navigation bars**, creative **assets**, and **styles** for you to use. Full-size and mobile-friendly templates, along with lots of ready-made content, mean anyone can publish a professional-looking website, no prior experience required! You'll also be able to reuse your existing content by importing word processing documents, images, and many other files.

To make the most of pictures in your site you can use **Cutout Studio** to remove backgrounds and **PhotoLab** for powerful image adjustment and effect combinations. You simply cannot afford to miss them!

WebPlus X7 doesn't just stop at "static" web publishing. The real power comes when adding and managing dynamic or interactive content, such as **forms**, **blogs**, **forums**, **video playlists**, and third-party RSS feeds. Also add modern essentials such as **panels**, **sliders**, and **Google Maps**, plus **Facebook**, **Twitter**, and **Google+** widgets. You can even make use of easy **e-commerce tools** with step-by-step setup for shopping cart and donation features.

Once you're happy with your WebPlus site, simply **publish to the web** to share with business colleagues, customers, friends and family alike.

Registration

Don't forget to register your new copy, using the **Registration Wizard**, on the **Help** menu. That way, we can keep you informed of new developments and future upgrades!

This User Guide

The WebPlus X7 User Guide is provided for the new or inexperienced user to get the very best out of WebPlus. As the program is packed with a wealth of features, this User Guide doesn't cover all product functionality, but instead focuses on core and frequently used features. For comprehensive assistance, please use WebPlus Help (press your F1 key).

New features

Based on a very strong and richly-featured website builder, the latest version of WebPlus brings a range of innovations and improvements to make your sites more modern, more professional looking and more interactive, while providing a streamlined and more efficient working environment.

- **HTML5 websites**
  Websites you create with WebPlus X7 will use the newest Internet standard, HTML5—so they'll look great and be fast in all the latest desktop and mobile browsers.

- **64-bit operation for improved performance**
  WebPlus is fully optimized for operation on 64-bit computers, and will automatically install a 64-bit version if appropriate.

Ease of Use

- **Feed-based Startup Assistant** (see p. 11)
  The fresh, new starting point for your web design provides a wealth of constantly-updating news items and WebPlus-specific learning resources (video tutorials, written tutorials, help, tips and tricks).

- **Improved assets available throughout your design** (see p. 137)
  Save more objects as assets to make videos and other media, code fragments, colour schemes and more, easy to reuse. You can access all your assets in many more places, choosing buttons as controls, pictures for your rollovers, and others throughout the design process.

- **Save and reuse object settings and behaviours** (see p. 145)
  Objects that have interactivity, like buttons, sliders, forms, e-commerce objects, video players with your choice of playlist controls etc. can have their options, settings or behaviours saved for applying to other objects.

Media and Interactivity

- **Video Player** (see p. 109)
  Add **videos** compatible with all the latest browsers and mobile devices, without your website visitors needing a Flash plug-in or media playing software!

- **Form designer** (see p. 119)
  Create your own forms with new drag and drop simplicity; no programming required. Add smart modules comprised of labels and one or more fields, rearrange within an intelligent layout, and choose a style.

- **Accommodation booker** (see p. 164)
  This new **Smart Object** gives hoteliers and other accommodation managers a neat way to offer online booking, with availability checking, confirmation emails, and rate periods, for any number of rooms, room types, plots, etc.

- **YouTube playlists and Vimeo videos** (see p. 113, p. 114)
  Now add streaming Vimeo videos to your site, and improve your YouTube video offerings with playlists—whether they're YouTube playlists, a list based on search results, a channel's uploads, or a playlist you compile yourself.

Improved Output

- **New HTML output options**
  In addition to brand new HTML5 export that makes WebPlus sites more efficient and compatible than ever, new site options allow you to choose the style and efficiency of code for the editor view, when previewing, and when publishing.

- **Export Optimizer**
  Save pictures from WebPlus, selecting objects, areas, or pages to export as optimized images that give you an interactive preview with file size estimate.

- **CSS styling** (see p. 172)
  New options available for almost all objects allows style settings to be added that are drawn by the viewer's web browsers, so more styling is available as efficient code.

WebPlus Help lists additional minor product improvements on previous versions. See the New Features topic in WebPlus Help for more details.

Installation

Installing WebPlus follows different procedures depending on whether you are installing from disc or via download.

You can install your new version alongside previous versions and use them independently.

32 or 64-bit WebPlus X7 installs to respective 32 or 64-bit computers.

Installation procedure (from disc)

- Insert your purchased disc into your disc drive.

    - If AutoPlay is enabled on the drive, this automatically starts the Setup Wizard. Follow the on-screen instructions to install WebPlus.

        -or-

    - If AutoPlay is not enabled (or doesn't start the install automatically), navigate to your program disc and double-click **autorun.exe**.

Installation procedure (from download)

- From **serif.com**, when logged into your Serif account, follow the on-screen instructions to download.

System Requirements

Minimum:

- Windows-based PC* with DVD drive and mouse

- Operating systems:
  Microsoft Windows® XP SP3 (32 bit)
  Windows® Vista (32 or 64 bit)
  Windows® 7 (32 or 64 bit)
  Windows® 8 (32 or 64 bit)

- 1GB RAM

- 340MB free hard disk space

- 1024 x 768 monitor resolution (at 100% display resolution)

- Internet Explorer 8

- Internet connection required for publishing to web and accessing online resources

* Main processor must support SSE2 instructions.

Recommended:

As for Minimum but:

- 560MB free hard disk space.

- Additional disk resources and memory are required when editing large and/or complex sites.

Optional:

- Internet Explorer 9 (for better HTML5 compatibility)

- Windows-compatible printer

- TWAIN-compatible scanner and/or digital camera

- .NET 2.0 for text import filters (Word 2007/2010 + OpenOffice) (installed by default; for Windows 8, an extra 1GB of free hard disk space is required).

Setting up Sites and Pages

2

Startup Assistant

Once WebPlus has been installed, you're ready to start.

- For Windows Vista/7: Setup adds a **Serif WebPlus X7** item to the **All Programs** submenu of the Windows **Start** menu. Use the Windows **Start** button to pop up the Start menu, click on **All Programs** and then click **Serif WebPlus X7**.

- For Windows 8: The Setup routine during install adds a **Serif WebPlus X7** entry to the desktop. Double-click the WebPlus icon from the desktop, or if the desktop is hidden, click the Windows **Start** button to display it.

On program launch, the Startup Assistant is displayed which offers different routes into WebPlus.

The options are described as follows:

The default home page keeps you in touch with Serif promotions and showcases articles (tutorials, etc.) You can also view the Overview and Quick Start video.

To access WebPlus files; also provides recent file history.

For online video/written tutorials, help, tips & tricks, and more—all via an updating feed that can be filtered by article Type. The Product Help and your electronic WebPlus X7 user guide are also provided.

Creates a new website from scratch, using a simple setup.

Creates an instant website from a pre-designed template.

For cross-product news, company news, articles, and product announcements, using Serif's news feed.

Any time you access the Startup Assistant, the Learn or News buttons indicate the number of new articles to be viewed (if available). This number will decrease as you read each article in the Learn or News pane. When new articles arrive, these will be indicated the next time you open the Startup Assistant.

Any new unread article arriving in the Learn or News pane will display a "new" indicator in its thumbnail.

Once you've clicked on a new article the "new" indicator changes to a "read" indicator (   ).

Don't forget to use the keyword Search box at the top-right of the Startup Assistant.

This is an incredibly powerful tool for filtering specific website names, Learn articles, theme layout names, or news articles.

To access the Startup Assistant when WebPlus is already running, select **Startup Assistant** from the **File** menu.

Creating a site using a design template

WebPlus comes complete with a whole range of categorized design templates which will speed you through the creation of all kinds of websites.

Each template offers:

- **Complementary design**—Professionally designed layout with high-visual impact.

- **Schemes**—choose a named colour scheme to apply a specific look and feel.

- **Page selection**—select some or all template pages (e.g., Home, Products, About Us, etc.) to base your new site on.

Design templates come in two types—**theme layouts** and ready-to-go **Pro templates**.

Theme layouts

These offer a choice of themes (e.g., Eco, Pop, Prospectus, and 27 more) on which to base your site. Simply add your own pictures to placeholders and personalize placeholder titles and text, then publish.

Ready-to-go Pro templates

These are categorized templates containing royalty-free pictures and catchy titles which can be adopted to fast-track you to your completed website. You just need to personalize placeholder text, and then publish.

Equivalent mobile-ready layouts are available for both theme layouts and Pro templates—these can be used to create your own site optimized for smart phone access.

To create a site using a design template:

1.   Open WebPlus, or select **Startup Assistant** from the **File** menu.

2.   Click **Templates**.

3.   From the left-hand pane, select a desktop or mobile option from Theme Layouts or WebPlus X7 Pro Templates categories.

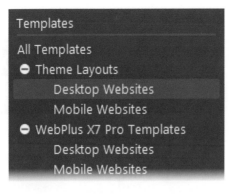

4.   Navigate the main pane by scrolling using the right-hand scroll bar.

5.   Select a thumbnail design you like from the main pane.

Theme Layout (Desktop)

Theme Layout (Mobile)

Pro Design Template (Desktop)

Pro Design Template (Mobile)

6. From the right-hand pane, decide which pages you wish to be part of your site. Check or uncheck under each page to select or deselect, respectively.

7. Pick a **Colour Scheme** from the drop-down list at the top of the dialog (the first three schemes are designed specifically for the chosen template). With the drop-down list open, you can preview your pages as you scroll through the schemes by using your keyboard up/down arrow keys. The page thumbnails will refresh to reflect the new page's appearance.

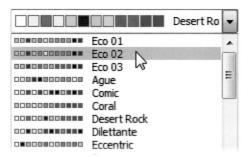

(Optional) Use the BACK button if you want to alter your choices.

8. Click **OK**. The pages are added to your new site.

Starting a site from scratch

Although **design templates** (p. 13) can simplify your design choices, you can just as easily start out from scratch with a new, blank site. Your site is created via the **Startup Assistant** which helps cover the key aspects of your site's creation.

Create	
Site Name	Villereccio Pizzeria
Site URL	http://villereccio.com/
Colour Scheme	▢▮▮▮▮▮▮▮▮▮▢ Default ▾ …
Default Page Size	960x1000 (Desktop) ▾
Initial Number of Pages	5
Add a Navigation Bar	☑
Save Site	☑

Start new site

The page size and height will be identical for all pages, including a master page that also gets created and assigned to every new page. A default navigation bar is added to this master page automatically.

To start a new site from scratch (via Startup Assistant):

1. Open WebPlus to display the **Startup Assistant**.
   - or -
   Select **Startup Assistant** from the **File** menu (during your session).

2. Select **New Site**.

3. Complete the details in the displayed main pane.

4. Click **Start new site**. Your site is created, ready for editing.

At this stage and subsequently, Site Properties can be edited to fine-tune your site settings. Select **Site Properties** (Publishing) via the **Properties** menu.

> From the Startup Assistant, you can press the **Esc** key to open a blank publication using default page properties.

To start a new blank site during your WebPlus session:

•   During your WebPlus session, click ⬜ **New Site** on the **Standard** toolbar.

The new site opens with a blank page using default **site properties**.

Opening an existing site

You can open an existing WebPlus site from the **Startup Assistant**, **Standard** toolbar, or via the **File** menu.

It is also possible to **import web pages** from existing HTML websites via the **File** menu. (See WebPlus Help for more details.)

1. Open WebPlus to display the initial **Startup Assistant**.
   - or -

   Select **Startup Assistant** from the **File** menu (during your session).

2. Select **Open**.

3. Several options are possible:

   i. For recently opened sites, select a thumbnail from the main pane.

- or -

    i.   For other WebPlus sites, select **WebPlus files** from the Browse My Computer pane.

    ii.   From the dialog, locate and select your file, then click **Open**.

To open existing WebPlus sites (during WebPlus session):

1. Click  **Open** on the **Standard** toolbar.

2. In the **Open** dialog, select the folder and file name(s). For multiple sites, **Shift**-click to select adjacent multiple files or **Ctrl**-click to select non-adjacent files.

3. Click the **Open** button.

To open sites by drag-and-drop:

- From Windows Explorer, drag and drop the site's preview thumbnail anywhere onto the WebPlus workspace.

To revert to the saved version of an open site:

- Choose **Revert** from the **File** menu.

Understanding site structure

The "structure" of a website has nothing to do with its physical layout, or where pages are stored. Rather, it's a way of logically arranging the content on the site so that visitors have an easier time navigating through it. One of the most useful organizing principles—which WebPlus strongly reinforces—is an "inverted tree" structure that starts with the Home page and then branches out to other pages. To the visitor navigating your site, this arrangement presents your content in a familiar, hierarchical way, structured into **sections** and **levels**.

- A **section** is a content category, each being a separate page, e.g. "Home, "About Us", "Gallery", "Products", and "Contact".

- The **level** is the number of steps (i.e., jumps) a given page is removed from its "parent" page. The Home page will always reside at Level 1, normally along with "section" pages. This allows navigation bars to work easily and automatically. Pages one step below the "section" pages reside at Level 2, and are considered to be child pages of the "parent" page.

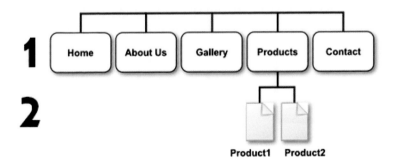

Viewing site structure

Two ways of viewing the site structure are possible: via the Site tab or via the **Site Structure View**. The latter is ideal for viewing larger sites.

Via Site tab

In WebPlus, the Site Structure tree (in the Site tab) provides a visual aid that lets you organize the content on your site into sections and levels. Here's how the above structure might appear:

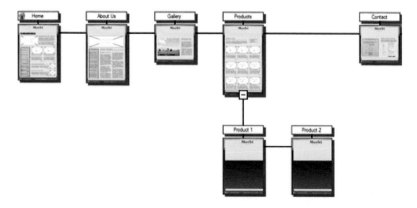

Via Site Structure View

For larger websites, **Site Structure view** can be used instead of the Site tab to provide a full-screen display that previews your "section and level" site structure as page thumbnails presented in a tree-based structure.

To view your site structure:

• From the **Standard** toolbar, select ⊞ **View Site Structure**.

The toolbar also lets you show and preview pages, include/exclude pages in navigation, rearrange pages by drag-and-drop, and even Quick Publish the selected page(s).

Setting site properties

Site properties allow settings to be made which will be applied across the entire site. Generally speaking, important site properties (page width, height, etc.) are automatically set on selecting a **template** or when **starting from scratch**. Other settings do not normally need to be modified (although you can at any time).

Some site properties such as page appearance and search-engine optimization settings are also mirrored on individual pages (via **Page Properties**). This lets you override or complement the "global" Site Properties, respectively, and apply "local" settings to specific pages.

To get you up to speed quickly on the various options, we've included a summary table below showing key Site property settings, with links to relevant topic coverage.

To view or change site property settings:

• Choose **Site Properties** from the **Properties** menu. The Site Properties dialog appears, with each displayed menu option reflecting an aspect of site properties.

Setting page properties

Your WebPlus site has its own general framework, consisting of the **site** itself; one or more **master pages**; and a number of individual **pages**. Each aspect of the framework has various **property** settings that contribute to the look and behaviour or your site when it's published. Whether you start with a WebPlus template or from scratch, you can choose whether to stick with the default property settings or alter them to suit your needs.

To view or change page (master page) property settings:

* Right-click the active page and select **Page Properties**.

Understanding pages and master pages

Looking at individual pages from a design standpoint, each WebPlus page has a "foreground" **page** and a "background" **master page**.

Master pages provide a flexible way to store background elements that you would like to appear on more than one page—for example a logo, background, header/footer, border design, or navigation bar. The key concept here is that a particular master page is typically shared by multiple pages, as illustrated below. By placing a design element on a master page and then assigning several pages to use that master page, you ensure that all the pages incorporate that element. Of course, each individual page can have its own elements.

The **Site tab** includes an upper Master Pages section containing your master page(s), and a lower Site Structure in the Pages window containing your standard pages. Each page shown in the window indicates the master page being used for that page.

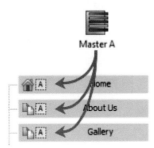

For more varied page designs across your site, you can **create** more than one master page (see **Adding, removing, and rearranging pages** on p. 27). Once you have multiple master pages, they can be **attached to separate pages** or **in combination on the same page**.

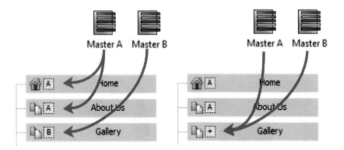

Attaching different master pages

By default, pages created in new sites have a master page (e.g., Master A) automatically attached to them. However, if your site has more than one master page you can attach a different master page to the page instead.

To attach a different master page to a page:

1. In the Site tab, right-click the page and select **Page Properties**.

2. From the dialog's Master Pages menu option, uncheck the original master page, then check the master page you want to use.

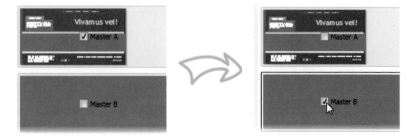

3. Click **OK**.

To detach a master page:

- Uncheck its entry in the **Page Properties** dialog (Master Page menu option).

> Unchecking all master pages means that the page will use the site appearance **(Properties>Site Properties)**.

> For more complex page designs, you can apply multiple master pages to your page at the same time. See *Attaching multiple master pages* in WebPlus Help.

Adding, deleting, and rearranging pages

Using the **Site** tab, you can:

- **Add** pages.

- **Delete** pages.

- Add one or more **master pages**.

- Use drag-and-drop to **rearrange** pages within your site structure.

- Add pages from design **templates**.

- Add **offsite links**.

- Add **HTML pages**.

- Set a page to be the **home page**.

Use the upper Master Pages window of the Site tab to access master pages, and the Pages window to access pages.

Adding pages

To add a new blank page:

1. In the Pages Window of the **Site** tab, select a page after which you want to add the new page.

2. Click the down arrow on the  **Add** button directly above the window. From the drop-down menu, choose **New Blank Page**.

3. In the **Page Properties** dialog, specify options for the new page from each of the menu options in turn.

4. Click **OK**.

A new page appears at the specified location in the site structure.

> Any new page created will use the currently set **Site Properties** (**Properties** menu), such as the default page size and alignment, but you can overwrite site properties by editing **Page Properties**.

Adding master pages

To add a new master page:

1. On the **Site** tab, ensure the **Master Pages**> button is clicked to expand the Master Page Window.

2. Click the **Add** button above the Master Pages window. A new master page appears in the **Site** tab's Master Pages window.

To reassign pages to particular master pages, see **Understanding pages and master pages** on p. 24.

Deleting pages

To delete a selected page or master page:

•   Click ▤ **Delete selected page** above the appropriate window.

Creating HTML pages

HTML pages can be added to any Site tab's Site Structure. See Creating HTML pages in WebPlus Help for more information.

Rearranging pages

You can also use the Site tab to rearrange pages as needed.

To move a page:

•   From the **Site** tab, drag the page entry up or down and drop it at a new position in the Site Structure tree.

    ⌐▤ moves the page to the same level as, and following, the highlighted target page.

    ▭⌐▤ makes the page a child of the page below the highlighted target page.

Adding template pages

While adding a blank page gives you page design freedom, you can make life a little easier by adopting "ready to go" template pages. You can select template pages that complement your existing theme layout or choose an independent template page.

This is possible by selecting **New Template Page** on the **Site** tab's **Add new page or link** drop-down list.

Adding offsite links

You can also add an **offsite link** to your site structure. Typically, this would be a page or resource (e.g. a blog or forum) separate from your site that you wanted to include in your site's navigation structure. The offsite link appears in the Site Structure tree and in navigation bars.

The **New Offsite Link** on the **Site** tab's **Add new page or link** drop-down list allows you to do this.

Setting your home page

To make a web page your home page:

- Right-click on a standard page in your Site tab then select **Set as Home Page**.

Layout Items

3

Inserting text frames

Typically, text in WebPlus goes into **text frames**, which work equally well as containers for single words or standalone paragraphs and articles. You can also use **artistic text** (see p. 131) for standalone text with special effects, or **table text** (see **Inserting tables** on p. 49) for row-and-column displays.

Creating text frames

You add frames to a page as you would any other object.

You can select, move, and resize any frame, but you cannot alter its basic shape. (See WebPlus Help for more information.)

When you resize a text frame, its story text reflows to the new dimensions.

To create a frame:

1. On the **Quick Build** tab (Layout Items category), click [T] **Text Frame**.

2. Drag out to place the text frame at your chosen dimensions.
   - or -

   Click on the page or pasteboard to create a new frame at a default size.

Putting text into a frame

You can put text into a frame in one of several ways.

WritePlus story editor:	With a selected frame, click **WritePlus** on the Frame context toolbar.
Importing text:	Right-click on a frame and choose **Insert>Text File** to import text.
Typing into the frame:	Select the Pointer Tool, then click for an insertion point to type text straight into a frame, or edit existing text. (See **Editing text on the page** on p. 132.)
Pasting via the Clipboard:	At an insertion point in the text, press **Ctrl+V**.

Controlling overflowing frame text

Fitting story text precisely into text frames is part of the art of laying out websites. If there's too much story text to fit in your text frame, WebPlus stores it in an **overflow area** hidden from view (but not lost!) at the bottom of the frame.

The **Text overflow** button displays under the overflowing frame to indicate this hidden text, so it's important to ensure the text is made to display again, otherwise your story will remain truncated.

To do this, several options are open to you:

- Physically resize your text frame if you have space.

- Consider rewriting your story, making it more concise!

- Resize your text.

To resize frame text once frames are sized and positioned, various text sizing and AutoFit options are available on the Frame context toolbar.

> You can apply a border to your text frame and adjust the padding between the text and the border by editing the text frame's CSS Properties. For more information, see WebPlus Help.

Inserting pictures

The **Assets** tab (Pictures category) acts as a "basket" for initially gathering together and then including pictures in your site. Its chief use is to aid the design process by improving efficiency (avoiding having to import pictures one by one) and convenience (making pictures always-at-hand).

WebPlus also lets you **insert pictures** from the **Quick Build** tab or **Basic** toolbar.

Adding pictures to the Assets tab

To add pictures to the tab:

1. Select the **Assets** tab's Pictures category, and click **Add**.

2. From the dialog, navigate to a folder, and select your picture(s).

3. Click **Open**. Your pictures appear as thumbnails within the **Assets** tab's Pictures category.

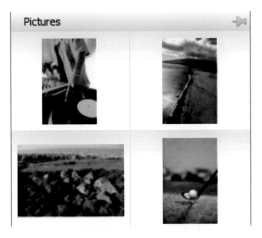

To reorder pictures in the tab:

● Select and drag a picture to a new position in the tab.

To delete a picture from the tab:

● Right-click a picture and select **Delete Asset**.

Adding pictures to the page

Pictures can be added to your site by dragging directly onto your page.

To add a picture to your page:

● From the **Assets** tab (Pictures category), drag a picture thumbnail directly onto the page, inline into artistic/frame text (at a chosen insertion point), or into a placeholder/populated picture frame.

Once added, the picture thumbnail indicates the number of times the picture has been used in the site ( ).

Placed pictures are linked to your project by default and not embedded.

Photos can be embedded using **Insert Picture From Disk** on the **Basic** toolbar (select **Embed Picture** at the bottom of the dialog) or at any time using the Resource Manager (see WebPlus Help).

Replacing pictures

You can swap a picture at any time, especially useful when you want to retain the position and dimensions on the page but want to update the picture itself. It can be used on any image (uncropped or cropped).

To replace a picture:

1. Click **Replace Picture from Disk** or **Replace Picture from Assets** directly under the selected picture. This sources pictures from anywhere on your computer or from a supplied (or custom) Asset Pack, respectively.

2. Use the **Import Picture** dialog to select the picture to open.

3. Click **Open**.

 You can also replace a picture with those stored in the Asset Browser—click **Replace Picture from Assets** directly under the selected picture.

Displaying pictures in lightboxes

Lightboxes are a simple way of displaying pop-up larger sized versions of pictures from thumbnails you add to your web page. A great advantage of lightboxes is that bigger pictures can be displayed on demand and are superimposed over your web page after a gliding animation.

To create a lightbox for a picture on your web page:

1. Select the picture (preferably a thumbnail).

2. Create a **hyperlink** to it (click **Hyperlink** from the **Properties** menu).

3. Select **Picture** from the menu, then from the **Target Window** tab, choose **Lightbox** from the **Type** drop-down list.

Cutting out pictures

Cutout Studio offers a powerful integrated solution for cutting objects out from their backgrounds. Depending on the make up of your pictures you can separate subject of interests from their backgrounds, either by retaining the subject of interest (usually people, objects, etc.) or removing a simple uniform background (e.g., sky, studio backdrop). In both instances, the resulting "cutout" image creates an eye-catching look for your site.

To launch Cutout Studio:

1. Select an image to be cut out.

2. Select  **Cutout Studio** from the displayed Picture context toolbar. Cutout Studio is launched.

3. Click either **Keep brush** or **Discard brush** from the left of the Studio workspace, and paint regions to be kept or discarded. Follow the Help pane in the studio for more detailed information.

Picture adjustments and effects

PhotoLab is a powerful studio for applying adjustment and effect filters
to pictures, either individually or in combination!

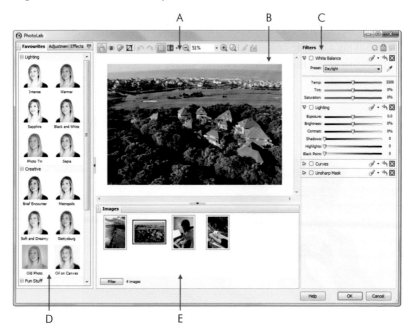

*(**A**) main toolbar, (**B**) main workspace, (**C**) filter stack, (**D**) filter tabs, (**E**)
Images tab*

To apply adjustments or effects in PhotoLab:

1. Select the picture that you want to apply a filter to.

2. Click 🔘 **PhotoLab** on the Picture context toolbar.

3. Select a filter from the filter tabs (Favourites, Adjustments, or
    Effects).

4. 🔘 Adjust the filter's settings to your liking in the lower-right **Trial
    Zone**, then click **Commit**.

5.   Repeat for additional filters.

6.   Click **OK**.

For more information, see WebPlus Help.

Inserting panels

Panels are information boxes superimposed over your web page, which can host pictures and text (below), as well as shapes and line art.

Vestibulum velit orci

Nulla vestibulum eleifend nulla. Suspendisse potenti. Aliquam turpis nisi, venenatis non, accumsan nec, imperdiet laoreet, lacus.

Maecenas condimentum tincidunt lorem. Vestibulum vel tellus. Sed vulputate. Morbi massa nunc, convallis a, commodo gravida, tincidunt sed,

The ability to superimpose panels means that you can increase the amount of information available to the web visitor without altering the underlying web page content. Panels can also be made to display only when required as you click or roll over **buttons**, pictures, or other **assets**. They can also be made to display permanently—great for navigation bars that never disappear on window scrolling!

Panels are also used as building blocks for creating animated **sliders** (p. 53). Like revolving advertising hoardings around sports stadiums, sliders can be made to change which panel is displayed at set time intervals.

WebPlus provides a wide selection of modern backgrounds to base your panel on. Alternatively, you can customize a background preset further or create a panel background from scratch in WebPlus's **Design Studio**. See WebPlus Help for more information.

Inserting your panel

To insert a panel:

1. From the **Quick Build** tab (Layout Items category), click
    Panel.

2. Drag the cursor across your page to define the size and shape of your panel region.

The **Insert Panel** dialog opens.

3. In the **Panel** tab:

    • Click the panel preview box.

    • In the **Asset Browser**, select page content on which to base your background and click **OK**.
       The preview box updates with your chosen panel design.

4. Click **OK**.

A panel of default size can be created by dragging from the **Quick Build** tab directly onto the page. Alternatively, a default basic panel (without editing via dialog) can be created by **Ctrl**-dragging to the page.

To edit a panel:

- Double-click the panel and edit the panel settings.

Adding content to your panel

You should treat your panel as an empty building block which can be developed using WebPlus tools and features. By creating objects within the panel area, they belong to the panel. This extends to objects such as text frames, artistic text, tables, QuickShapes, and pictures. Dragging the panel will also move its associated objects.

Hiding/showing your panel

Why would you want to hide your panel once you've designed it? The power of panels comes with their ability to be hidden and then be shown as a result of rolling over or clicking a page object. This means that buttons, pictures, and gallery objects can reveal more detailed information only when needed.

To allow this to happen, the object has to be "brought to life", i.e. by assigning it an **action** (p. 71) that is triggered in response to a rollover or click. The action also connects the already created panel to the object.

To assign an action to a panel:

1. Select the panel.

2. From the context toolbar, select ⚙️ **Actions**.

    The **Edit Panel** dialog opens, displaying the **Actions** tab.

3. Click **Add** and choose **Visibility** from the flyout.

4. Select the panel from the **Object ID** drop-down list.

5. Select an event from the **Event** drop-down list.

    The event relates to the behaviour that occurs when you perform an action (i.e., when you click or rollover the object).

Object ID:	panel_1 ▼
Event:	Show on rollover; hide on rollout ▼
☑ Fade	
Speed: △	150 ms

6. Click **OK**.

Finally, the panel can be hidden with a single click once you've finished designing it.

To hide a selected panel:

●   From the context toolbar, select 🔲 **Show or Hide the object**.

> 🔹 To toggle the visibility of hidden objects as you design, from the **View** menu, select **Hidden Objects**.

On publishing your page, a rollover of the page object will display the panel.

It's possible to create custom panel backgrounds by using WebPlus's Design Studio. See WebPlus help for more information.

Inserting a Photo Gallery

In WebPlus you can add a Flash™- or JavaScript-based photo gallery to any web page, using one of a range of eye-catching gallery types, styles, and a choice of photo navigation methods.

Gallery types

Different Flash or JavaScript gallery types can be used to create your Photo Gallery.

Gallery type	Features

Professional Flash Photo Gallery

Provides a top or bottom control bar (hosting preview thumbnail rollovers) on top of your main photo display.

Professional Flash Photo Gallery (Live Feed)

As for Professional Flash Photo Gallery but photo content is sourced online from your **Flickr** photostream (as an RSS feed), another RSS 2.0-compatible image host, or SlideShowPro Director.

Flash Photo Gallery

Provides a top or bottom control bar on top of your main photo display which offers basic navigation control and/or scrollable horizontal/vertical preview thumbnail rollovers. Photo grids and photo stacks are also available. You can also accompany your photo gallery with background music.

JavaScript Photo Gallery

Like Flash Gallery but offers JavaScript-based photo galleries. Photo grids, photo stacks, and **lightboxes** are available.

Inserting a Photo Gallery

The Photo Gallery is inserted on the page, just like an individual photo, except that the currently displayed photo is surrounded by a background, navigation bar and preview thumbnails.

To insert a Photo Gallery:

1.   From the **Quick Build** tab (Layout Items category), click
     Photo Gallery.

2.   To insert the gallery at a default size, position the displayed
     cursor where you want the gallery to appear on the page, then
     simply click the mouse.
     - or -

     To set the size of the inserted gallery, drag out a region and release
     the mouse button.

3.   Select the **Gallery Type** as described on p. 45.

4.   Click **Next**.

To add photos to a Photo Gallery:

1.   For all Gallery types (except the Live Feed type) from the dialog,
     choose whether to:

     •   **Add individual files**
         Click the **Add Files** button to navigate to then select the photo
         file(s) to open. Use **Ctrl**-click or **Shift**-click to select multiple
         non-adjacent or adjacent files.
         - or –

     •   Click the **Add Assets** button to navigate to then select the
         photo file(s) to open.
         - or -

     •   **Add all photos in a folder**
         Click the **Add Folder** button to navigate to a folder then select
         it to add its content.

(Optional) Select any photo thumbnail(s) for manipulation.

- To add a caption, click the **Caption** column and input text, numbers and characters.

- (Professional Flash Photo Gallery only) To add hyperlinks to photos, click **Edit hyperlink**. From the dialog, choose a **Hyperlink Type**—you can set no hyperlink, hyperlinks to the original image, or hyperlinks to a different **link destination** (e.g., Site Page or Internet Page).

2. Click **Next**.

To select and modify a Photo Gallery style:

1. Select a style from the **Gallery Style** pane at the top of the dialog.

2. (Optional) For the selected style, use the pane on the right to modify various gallery-wide options (autoplay, background/frame/font colour, caption and navigation bar control, etc.).

3. Click **Finish**.

Editing the Photo Gallery

Once added to the web page, the Photo Gallery can be edited.

To edit a Photo Gallery:

1. Select a gallery already present on your web page.

2. Double-click the gallery. The **Photo Gallery** dialog is displayed. The options available are the same as those available when the gallery was created.

Once a gallery is placed on the page it's also possible to drag a corner of the gallery object to resize. Use the **Shift** key while dragging to maintain the aspect ratio.

Inserting tables

Tables are ideal for presenting text and data in a variety of easily customizable row-and-column formats, with built-in spreadsheet capabilities.

			£/€
Vivamus vel	345-56	1	4.24/4.97
Praesent nisl	334-B299	2	4.64/5.44
Mauris nibh	089-78	2	2.93/3.44
Nullam eleifend	455-13	1	7.10/8.32
Donec viverra	345-33	1	2.55/2.99

Each cell in a table behaves like a mini-frame. Like **frame text** you can vary character and paragraph properties, apply named text styles, embed inline images, apply solid text colour fills, and use proofing options such as Spell Checker and Proof Reader. Some unique features include number formatting and formula insertion.

Rather than starting from scratch, WebPlus is supplied with a selection of pre-defined table formats, i.e. templates, that can be used and edited. Simply pick one and fill in the cells with content.

To insert a table:

1. From the **Quick Build** tab (Layout Items category), click **Table**.

2. Click on your page, or drag out to set the size of your table.

The **Create Table** dialog appears with a selection of preset table formats shown in the **Format** window.

3. Step through the list to preview the layouts and select one (use up/down keyboard arrows for a "live" preview of each). To begin with a plain table, select (**Default**).

4. (Optional) Click **Edit** if you want to further customize your chosen format.

5. Set the **Table Size**. This is the number of rows and columns that make up the table layout.

6. Click **OK**. The new table appears on the page.

To modify the structure and cell contents of tables, please see Manipulating tables in WebPlus Help.

Inserting a calendar

The **Calendar Wizard** helps you design month-at-a-glance calendars for use on your web page.

December 2013						
M	T	W	T	F	S	S
30	31					1
2	3	4	5	6	7	8
9	10	11	12	13	14	15
16	17	18	19	20	21	22
23	24	25	26	27	28	29

The calendar is created as a scalable **text-based table** so you can edit text using the standard text tools. The properties of a selected calendar are similar to those of a table, and can be modified identically (see Manipulating tables in WebPlus Help).

The wizard lets you set up the month/year and calendar style/format, and controls the inclusion of personal events and/or public holidays.

To insert a calendar:

1. From the **Quick Build** tab (Layout Items category), click
    Calendar.

2. Click on your page, or drag out to set the size of your table.

3. From the displayed **Calendar Wizard**, define options for your calendar including setting the year and month, calendar style (square, or in single or multiple column format), week start day, display options, switching on personal events/holidays, and calendar format.

    To have your country's public holidays shown, check **Add public holidays** in the wizard and select a **Region** from the associated drop-down list. To add personal events, check **Add personal events** additionally.

4. Select a predefined calendar format or to begin with a plain table, select **(Default)**.

5. Click **Finish** to complete the wizard.

> If you plan to use your calendar in subsequent years, simply update the **Year** setting in **Tools>Set User Details**.

To view and edit a selected calendar's properties:

1.   Click the **Edit Calendar** button on the Calendar context toolbar.

2.   Choose an appropriate tab (Date, Style, Events, etc.) and make your modification, then press **OK**.

Right-click (with the **Calendar** option selected) also lets you select, insert, distribute, delete, and adjust widths/heights for rows (or columns), as well as autofit to cell contents, but take care not to corrupt your table formatting!

Adding personal events

You can complement your public holiday listings (e.g., Easter holidays) by adding personal events such as birthdays and business launches so that the events show up on your calendar—simply use the **Calendar Events** button on a selected calendar's context toolbar. Events show automatically on your calendar under the chosen date.

Inserting sliders

Sliders are a fun and exciting way to animate panels, and are ideal for a whole range of uses including advertising banners, news tickers and as alternative navigation bars.

Each slider is made up of a series of panels, with just one panel visible at any one time.

Each panel can show a mixture of pictures, text, and line/shape art. Like a slideshow, each panel can be made to appear automatically at set intervals, manually via navigation buttons, or at a set time.

Various **animation styles** can be used to control how each panel is displayed. You can pick from directional styles (e.g., Left to right, Top to bottom, etc.) as well as Medley (mixed styles), Accordion, Overlays, and Scroller styles. Time-based displays are also configurable so you could make each panel appear for a Start and End date (or time).

Pre-designed professional sliders are available from the **Asset Browser**, and are typically customized once on the page. Panels can be added, reordered, or deleted to create the slider of your choosing.

To insert a slider:

1. From the **Insert** menu, select **Slider** from the **Interactive Object** flyout.

2. In the **Asset Browser** dialog, in the main pane, select an individual slider and click **OK**.

3. Click once to place the slider on the page.

You can also add sliders to the page using the Assets tab (see WebPlus Help).

To select a slider:

●   From the **Objects** tab, select the **Slider** entry. You'll see the slider context toolbar appear above your workspace allowing you to edit the slider.

If you're editing the contents of a panel and need to select the panel itself, select **Edit>Select>Select Parent** (**Ctrl+R**). Subsequently, the parent slider can then be selected by choosing **Edit>Select>Select Parent** again.

The Asset Browser also provides some sliders which have a separate supporting navigation bar for moving between panels. Simply modify each slider panel, to customize its look and feel.

Editing your slider

Your slider comes with a set of panels by default. It's likely that you'll want to:

- **Add**, **copy**, or **delete a panel** within the slider.

- **Add content** to any currently visible panel. Remember that, like standalone panels, each panel in the slider can have any content added to it.

- **Swap a picture** for one of your own by clicking **Replace Picture** under the panel's picture.

- **Add hyperlinks** from a panel's pictures, buttons, or other objects to another destination (e.g. to a main product page per panel), that displays in a new window or lightbox.

- Change the **Animation style** depending on how panels are to animate.

In addition, the slider's panel order and playback controls can also be modified.

To add a new panel:

1. Select the slider.

2. From the context toolbar, select **Add Panel**.

A blank panel is added at the end of the last panel in your slider. You can then **add content to your panel** (see p. 41).

> You can reorder panels within your slider via the toolbar's **Edit Slider** option.

To navigate between panels:

- Click the ◀ ▶ navigation buttons directly under the selected slider.

Every slider also has a Foreground panel that displays its contents permanently. The panel is perfect for adding contact details, sale buttons, telephone numbers, or a picture that you always want to show.

The slider properties can be modified to change the animation style and various playback controls. Panels within the slider can also be reordered and made to display at set times.

To modify slider properties:

1. Double-click the slider.

2. From the **Options** tab, select a style from the **Animation style** drop-down list. The lower window will automatically preview the new style once chosen.

3. Select other playback controls using check boxes or drop-down lists.

4. From the **Panels** tab, you can **Add Panel**, **Copy Panel**, **Delete Panel**, or rearrange panel order by drag and drop (or by using **Panel Left/Panel Right**). Enter a new **Name** to uniquely identify each panel, and/or change its **Background Colour**.

5. If the Animation style (in Options tab) is set to "Date & Time", enter a **Start Date**, **End Date**, **Start Time**, and **End Time** for each selected panel (except foreground panel).

6. Click **OK**.

Navigation
Items

Inserting navigation bars

Navigation bars are used to allow the site visitor to jump between pages serving different purposes, e.g. Home page, Gallery, Products, and Contact Us. They are automatically programmed to understand your **site structure** (see p. 21), making it easy to design a site that's simple to navigate.

Technically, navigation bars facilitate movement between the various **sections and levels** of a site, providing links to your Home page and other top-level section pages, while pop-up menus link to child pages within each section.

You can easily install navigation bars at any level of your site, reconfigure them to link to a particular part of the site, change the appearance of the navigation bar, and exclude particular pages from navigation as needed.

Inserting navigation bars

Navigation bars can be added to any page but are typically added to the **master page**—as this saves you the trouble of pasting the same element to multiple pages.

When inserting a navigation bar, you can choose how your navigation will appear on your page by choosing:

- **Type**: The intrinsic design of your navigation bar (e.g., designer, graphical, simple).

- **Navigation Type**: The site or custom structure on which the navigation bar is based.

- **Appearance**: The button, separator, and background design of the navigation bar. Either preset or custom designs can be used.

- **Pop-Up Menus**: The design of the text-based or button-based pop-up menu displaying off the navigation bar (if using child pages in your site structure).

- **ID/Anchor**: The HTML ID for the navbar object and the object's anchor can be set.

- **CSS Properties**: Some navigation bars can have CSS styling applied, e.g. a border. See **CSS properties** on p. 172.

- **Actions**: An action (change in Z-order, opacity, or custom) can be applied as a result of an event (mouse over). See **Applying actions** on p. 71.

To insert a navigation bar:

1. Select the page (or master page).

2. From the **Quick Build** tab (Navigation Items), click **Navigation Bar**.

3. Position your cursor and click at the point where you want your navigation bar to be placed (the bar will be aligned to the right of this point).

4. From the dialog's **Type** tab, browse navigation bar categories, clicking ⊞ to expand if necessary.

5. Review each navigation bar in turn (or scroll through the bars using the keyboard arrows for quick browsing)! Select your chosen navigation type, e.g. Tabs 2.

   - or -

   Click the **Browse Assets** button to see previews of all navigation bars in the asset browser. Select an item and click **OK** to return to the dialog.

6. From the **Navigation Type** tab choose whether to base your navigation bar directly on the site's **Site Structure** (enable **Based on site structure**)—an example site structure taken from the program's Site tab is shown below.

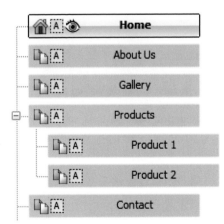

   - or -

   Customize the navigation bar's options (enable **Custom**).

If choosing **Based on site structure**, you can:

- Select the level of pages that will be included in the navigation bar: **Top Level**, **Parent Level**, **Same Level**, etc.

- Depending on the main selection, you can opt to include the **child pages**, **anchors**, **home page**, **parent page,** and/or **Hide current page** or **disabled links**.

- Set **Target Frame/Window** to change where the new page will open. Choose from **Same Window** (most common), **New Window** (useful for off-site pages), **Top of Current Window**, **Parent Frame**, **Named Window**, **Document Frame**, or **Lightbox**.

7. Click **OK**. The navigation bar appears on your page.

> Some navigation bars are colour schemed, allowing further control of the bar's appearance.

To edit a navigation bar:

1. Double-click the navigation bar.

2. Change settings available from each tab as described above.

It's also possible to customize navigation bars, buttons, separators, and backgrounds for your own navigation bar styles. See WebPlus Help.

Inserting pop-up menus

Pop-up menus form an integral part of multi-level **navigation bars** (p. 59), showing as menus that display only on button hover over. The items in pop-up menus represent child pages at lower levels of your site.

You can also add pop-up menus to any object (a QuickShape, image, a gallery item, but most typically a **button**), the menu being essentially the same as those integrated with navigation bars. Like navigation bars, the pop-up menu items that display can be configured, either adopting the entire site structure, just part of it, or your own custom structure.

You have full control of what level of your site you want to present in the pop-up menu. In the example opposite, the pop-up menu is based on child pages belonging to a Products parent page (which would probably host the button and pop-up menu).

To create a pop-up menu:

Select an object to attach the pop-up menu to.

1. From the **Properties** menu, select **Pop-Up Menu**.
   - or -

   Right-click an object and select **Pop-Up Menu**.

2. From the dialog's **Navigation Type** tab, check the **Show a pop-up menu of navigation links for this object** option to enable navigation from this object.

3. Enable **Based on site structure** or **Custom** to either use your site's navigation links as part of the menu or base the pop-up menu on your own **custom structure**, respectively. With the former, you can base your menu on child pages of a top-level "Products" page.

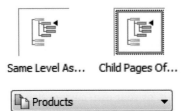

Same Level As...   Child Pages Of...

4. From the dialog's **Menu Appearance** tab, select **Text pop-up menus** or **Graphical pop-up menus**. The latter implements button objects to make up its menus.

5. Select a menu option from the box, then edit the values in input boxes, the choices in drop-down lists, select radio buttons, and check boxes to alter your pop-up menu design. Graphical pop-up menu settings for buttons, separators, and background share similar settings to those of buttons.

6. Click **OK**.

Inserting buttons

Buttons are an integral part of WebPlus **navigation bars** (see p. 59) but can also be added onto your web page, either standalone or as part of a form. When clicked by the web visitor, they can be made to display a **hyperlink destination**, **pop-up menu**, or trigger an **action**.

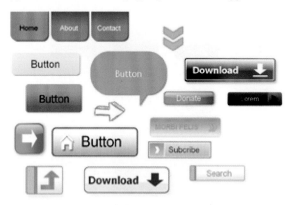

In WebPlus, buttons can be either a **preset design** or be **created from scratch** in the **Button Studio**. It's quite common to choose a preset and then customize it to fit your requirements (e.g., change the label text or its colour).

To insert a preset button:

1. From the **Quick Build** tab (Navigation Items category), click Abc **Button**.

2. Position your cursor and click at the point where you want your button to be placed. Alternatively, to set the size of the button, drag out a region and release the mouse button.

3. From the **Insert Button** dialog, click the button preview box.

4. From the **Asset Browser**, select a preset button type and click **OK**.

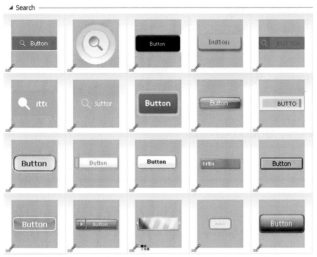

The preview box updates with your chosen button design.

5. Enter a **Button Label** to identify the button, such as "Home", "Images", etc. (available only for buttons that allow a text label).

6. From the Hyperlink tab:

    *   From the **Hyperlink Type** tab, select a link destination type which will direct the user to a target (e.g., Internet page, site page, file) via a **hyperlink** (see p. 67).

    *   From the **Target Window** tab, select a window or frame type from the Type drop-down list. For example, you could open the target page in a "New Window".

7. Click **OK**.

Additional tabs, called **Advanced** (Hyperlink tab) and **Actions**, offer accessibility and search engine relationship (REL) attributes, and a range of **actions** (p. 71) that can control user interactivity with your button. **ID/ Anchor** and **CSS Properties** tabs offer advanced controls and styling options.

For a range of website buttons and other graphical elements stored in Asset Packs, you can use the **Asset Browser**. From the **Assets** tab, click **Browse**, then select the Settings category.

To edit a button:

- Double-click a button and edit as described above.

Creating custom buttons

If you're looking to further modify your chosen button preset (or work from scratch) you can use **Button Studio**, a button design environment integrated into WebPlus. This allows you to focus on your button design without the distractions of other objects on the page, i.e. the design is displayed in isolation.

See WebPlus Help for more information.

To edit a button design:

- Select **Edit Button Design** from the context toolbar.

Adding hyperlinks and actions

Hyperlinking an object such as a box, some text, or a picture means that a visitor to your website can click on the object to trigger an event. The event is most commonly a jump to one of the following hyperlink targets:

- **Site page**

- **Internet page** (somewhere on the web)

- **Internet Email**

- **Anchor** (a designated target within a web page)

- **File on your local disk or network** (for download of files)

- **Shopping cart**

- **Smart object** (e.g., a forum, blog or CMS)

- **RSS feed** (or **podcast**)

- **Navigation element**

- **User Data**

- **Picture**

Actions are conceptually like hyperlinks, in that something happens on object click or rollover. They differ from hyperlinks in that a click or rollover produces an on-page user interaction with the object, rather than take you to a target destination. (See **Applying actions** on p. 71.)

Adding hyperlinks

To add a hyperlink:

1. Use the ![pointer] **Pointer Tool** to select the single or grouped object or highlight the region of text to be hyperlinked.

2. Select ![icon] **Hyperlink** from the **Properties** toolbar. The object's properties dialog appears.

3. On the **Hyperlink Type** tab (Hyperlink tab), click to select the link destination type, i.e. a Site Page, Internet Page, Smart Object, etc.

4. Depending on the link type, choose type-specific options in the right-hand pane.

5. Click **OK**.

> You can view and manage all hyperlinks and anchors throughout your site by using the **Site Manager**, accessible from the Default context toolbar (and **Tools** menu).

To modify or remove a hyperlink:

1. Use the ↖ **Pointer Tool** to select the object, or click for an insertion point inside the linked text. (It's not necessary to drag over a hyperlinked region of text.)

2. Select **Hyperlink** from the **Properties** toolbar.

The object's properties dialog appears with the current link target shown.

*   To modify the hyperlink, select a new link destination type, target, and/or options.

*   To remove the hyperlink, click **No Hyperlink**.

Selecting a target window

The **Target Window** tab offers a range of target windows, frames, or a
lightbox in which the link destination will be displayed.

To select a target window:

1.   From the object's properties dialog's **Hyperlink** tab, select the
     Target Window tab.

2.   Select an option from the **Type** drop-down list.

Selecting hyperlink appearance

For artistic, frame, or table text, several options exist in the dialog's
Appearance tab for how you want to derive your text hyperlink colours.

To change hyperlink appearance:

•   From the **Appearance** tab, use the **Style** drop-down list to choose
    how text hyperlink is formatted.

> The dialog's Advanced tab lets you choose various accessibility options
> such as **Access Keys** and **Title** names (shown as hover-over text
> describing the hyperlink destination).

To view or edit existing hyperlinks:

- From the **Tools** menu, select **Site Manager>Hyperlink Manager** to view, rename, or remove hyperlinks.

Applying actions

Actions can be associated with objects (not text) to allow for greater user interactivity. Available actions, triggered typically by a click or mouse rollover of the object, are as follows:

- **Alert**: Displays a pop-up alert box (on click).

- **Visibility**: Displays a **panel** (on rollover/click).

- **Opacity**: Makes objects transparent (until rollover), e.g. to only show navigation buttons on panel hover over.

- **Z-Index**: Changes the order (Z-index) of the object in relation to other objects (on rollover). A high Z-index value (e.g. 150) ensures the object appears in front of other objects on rollover. For example, a usually hidden picture in a picture stack can be promoted to the front on rollover.

- **Print**: Prints the current page via a Print dialog (on click).

- **Slider**: Adds an action (Play, Pause, etc.) to a supporting navigation button to control slider playback. You can add an appropriate action to each type of navigation buttons, i.e. a Play action can be applied to a Play button. (See **Sliders** on p. 53.)

- **Slider Feedback**: Changes the button state dynamically according to the slider's current playback state.

- **Custom**: Runs your own JavaScript code in response to a click, mouse, key press, and more.

The **Actions** tab is only displayed when you select an object (but not on text selection).

You'll need to create a panel in advance before you can assign an action to it, allowing it to display. For more information, see **Inserting panels** on p. 41.

To apply an action:

1. Select ⚙ **Edit Actions** from the **Properties** toolbar.

2. From the dialog, click **Add** and choose an option from the flyout.

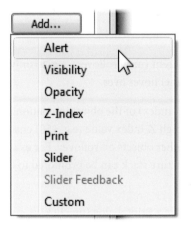

3. From the dialog, configure the action.

4. Click **OK**.

On previewing or publishing, a click or hover over of the object will trigger the action chosen.

Adding an anchor

An anchor is a specific location on a page that can serve as the **target** for a hyperlink (see p. 67). Invisible to the web page visitor, it typically marks a point within some text (such as the start of a particular section) or a picture at some point down the page.

To attach an anchor to a section of text:

1. Either:

    i. Use the Pointer Tool to click for an insertion point inside the target text.

    ii. From the Text menu, select **Insert>Anchor** (or press **Ctrl+Q**).
        - or -

    •   Right-click anywhere inside the target text and select **Insert>Anchor**.

2. The Anchor dialog opens. The anchor automatically adopts the name of the adjacent word in the target text.

3. (Optional) Rename the anchor using the Name of the anchor input box.

4. (Optional) Check Include Anchor in Navigation to allow the anchor to be accessed via a **navigation bar** instead of a hyperlink. You'll need to ensure Include anchors is checked on your **navigation bar settings** and that the anchor is given a title.

5. Click **OK**.

To insert an anchor to an object:

1. Use the **Pointer Tool** to select the target object.

2. Select **ID and Anchor** from the **Properties** toolbar.

3. In the dialog, select **Treat this object as an anchor**.

4. (Optional) To assign a specific anchor identification name to your anchor (rather than using the object's HTML ID), uncheck **Use object ID** and then type a name into the **Anchor ID** input box.

5. (Optional) Check **Include Anchor in Navigation**.

6. Click **OK**.

To view or edit existing anchors:

- From the **Tools** menu, select **Site Manager>Anchor Manager** to view, rename, or remove an anchor attached to a particular object. You can also include the anchor in page navigation.

Using lightboxes

Lightboxes are a fun and modern way of displaying all kinds of web content superimposed over your web page. When you click an object, the light box presents your chosen content "on demand" in a pop-up window.

Lightboxes can be used to display:

- Pictures, as a larger sized version of a picture thumbnail already added to your web page.

- Forms in your site.

- A login box for access control.

- Pages (Site or Internet).

- A blog, forum, or RSS feed.

- A Word file, PDF, or any other file type.

To create a lightbox for a picture on your web page:

1. Select the picture (preferably a thumbnail).

2. Click **Hyperlink** from the **Properties** toolbar.

3. From the **Hyperlink Type** tab, select **Picture** from the menu.

4. From the **Target Window** tab, choose **Lightbox** from the **Type** drop-down list.

5. (Optional) Add a caption to the picture in the lightbox using the **Caption** box. You can also make the picture part of a slideshow using the **Slideshow Name** drop-down list. (See **Lightbox slideshows** on p. 76.)

6. Click **OK**.

To restrict the display size of this linked "lightboxed" picture, WebPlus scales down outsized pictures to a maximum width and height (default 800 x 600 pixels) always preserving their aspect ratios. Images with native dimensions less than these maximum dimensions are left unchanged. The maximum width and height can be modified. (See **Setting site properties** on p. 23).

To create a lightbox to a local picture:

- As above but choose the **File** option instead of Picture.

You'll have the option to embed or link the picture; either way, the picture always displays using its native image dimensions.

Lightbox slideshows

Simple **lightbox slideshows** can be created which are based on the pictures already placed on the same web page. The lightbox itself will display controls to navigate through your slideshow.

To create a lightbox slideshow:

1. Create a lightbox for a picture on your web page (as above).

2. From the **Edit Picture** dialog's **Hyperlink** tab, select the **Target Window** tab.

3. Enter a slideshow name in the **Slideshow Name** drop-down list. This will be used for other pictures to be added to this slideshow. Click **OK**.

4. Repeat for the next picture. The previously created slideshow name will show for other pictures. Select the slideshow name to include this picture.

5. Click **OK**.

Lightboxes to any hyperlink target

Lightboxes are not just limited to the display of pictures. As a lightbox is actually a type of window, any **hyperlink target** (p. 68) can be displayed within it—typically a form, login box, page in your site, Internet page, blog, forum, or RSS feed. You can also view a Word file, PDF, or any other file type (using the **File** option) in your lightbox.

Interactive
Objects

5

Inserting rollover graphics

A picture whose appearance changes in response to a mouse event is called a **rollover graphic**. Mouse events could typically be a hover over or mouse button press.

> You can directly import rollover graphics created in Serif DrawPlus. (See WebPlus Help for more information.)

Rollover options

Creating rollovers is a matter of deciding which state(s) you'll want to define, then specifying a picture variant for each chosen state. WebPlus provides several choices:

Normal State
is the "resting" state
of the picture before
any rollover, and is
always defined.

Over State
is the state triggered
by a mouseover—
when the mouse
pointer is directly
over the picture.

Down State
is triggered by
clicking the mouse
then keeping the
button depressed
while on the picture.

> Another state, **Down+Over** (not illustrated) implies a mouseover that occurs when the picture is already Down, i.e. after it's been clicked.

You can also specify a **hyperlink** event—for example, a jump to a targeted web page—that will trigger if the user releases the mouse button while in down state. And you can even group buttons on a page so they work together—and only one button in the group can be 'down' at any one time.

To create a rollover graphic:

1. In a suitable image-editing program, create the variant source pictures for each state you'll be defining.

2. Click **Rollover** from the **Quick Build** tab (Interactive Objects) and drag the insert cursor across your page to set the rollover size.

3. In the Insert Rollover dialog, on the **Rollover Graphic** tab:

    *   Specify which rollover states (see above) you want to activate for each picture by checking boxes in the Rollover states section. For each one, use the **Browse** button to locate the corresponding source picture or click Browse Assets to locate pictures from your saved asset packs.

    *   (Optional) Specify **Export Options** for your pictures.

    *   Check **Embed files in site** if you want to incorporate the picture(s) in the site.

    *   Choose **Normal** or **Down** as the button's initial rollover state.

    *   Check **Radio button** if you want to link this rollover to others on its page (that have also got this option checked), so that only one is in a 'down' state at one time.

4. (Optional) On the **Hyperlinks** tab, define a hyperlink target for the rollover.

5. Click **OK**.

WebPlus displays the picture assigned to the Normal state. It's a good idea to **preview the page** and test each rollover picture, then return to WebPlus and revise as needed.

To edit a rollover graphic:

- Double-click the rollover graphic, to display the Edit Rollover dialog. Modify settings as appropriate.

Inserting pop-up rollovers

The most common use for pop-up rollovers in WebPlus is to hover over a picture thumbnail to show its larger representation, usually offset next to the thumbnail.

WebPlus lets you choose the position and size of the pop-up in relation to the "hovered over" thumbnail; even the thumbnail can be selected and resized at any time.

To insert a pop-up rollover:

1. Click **Pop-up Rollover** from the **Quick Build** tab (Interactive Objects) and drag the insert cursor across your page to set the rollover size.

2. From the **Edit Pop-Up Rollover** dialog, on the **Rollover Graphic** tab:

    -   For the Normal rollover image click the **Browse** button, and navigate to and select the image. Click **Open**.
        - or -
        Click the **Browse Assets** button and locate an image from your saved asset packs.

    -   For the Over image, the previously chosen Normal image is used by default (typically for photo thumbnails). However, you can **Browse** or **Browse Assets** to use a completely different image.

    -   (Optional) Specify an animation style and speed for the image popup.

    -   (Optional) Specify **Export Options**.

    -   (Optional) Check **Embed image files in site** if you want to incorporate the image(s) in the site.

3. (Optional) On the **Hyperlinks** tab, define a hyperlink target for the rollover.

4. Click **OK**.

If captioning is required on pop-up rollovers this can be made to appear next to your Over image (see WebPlus Help for details).

For pop-up rollovers to work effectively you'll need to position the Normal and Over images on your page. Positioning is carried out from a dedicated dialog, where each state image can be moved and resized by dragging (or by setting absolute pixel values). See WebPlus Help for more information.

To edit a pop-up rollover:

• Double-click the Normal image on the page, to display the **Edit Pop-Up Rollover** dialog. Modify settings as appropriate.

Inserting a site search

WebPlus uses a powerful search facility that matches user search terms with text that appears in your site in text frames or tables.

The search facility is created by combining a **Site Search Form** object with a **Site Search Results Frame**.

Site Search Results—creates a frame in which the search results are displayed. Typically, this is placed and sized onto its own page, and does not appear in the site navigation structure.

You'll normally position the search results frame ahead of adding the **Site Search Form**.

Site Search Form object—the text box in which users type the word or phrase they want to search for. This object is usually added to a master page and appears on all pages of the site.

The search results show a hyperlinked page name heading plus associated web page text for reference. Visitors simply click the hyperlink to access the web page.

To add Site Search Results:

1. Choose **Site Search** from the **Insert** menu and select **Site Search Results** from the submenu (placing your search results window on your page *after* configuring it).

    - or -

    Select **Site Search Results Frame** on the **Quick Build** tab (Interactive Objects) and drag the insert cursor across your page to place your search results window.

2. From the dialog, select various options to alter the appearance of results text and/or hyperlink text.

> Keep the search results on a separate, perhaps new, page which can also have its own look and feel (double-click the object to alter site results appearance).

To add a Site Search Form:

1. Choose **Site Search** from the **Insert** menu and select **Site Search Form** from the submenu.

2. Click the insert cursor to place your site search form object.

> Add the search object to the top of your master page to allow site-wide access to the search feature.

To edit the appearance of site search form or site search results frame:

*   Double-click the search object, to display its edit dialog. Modify settings as appropriate.

Inserting Google Maps

Use embedded **Google Maps** in your web page if want to make sure that a client can locate your headquarters, attendees can find that special meeting (or event), or identify any other special interest locations. Map, Street View, and Satellite views are available.

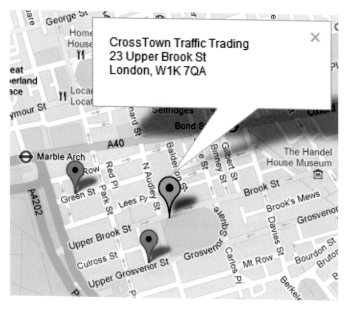

To insert a Google Map:

1. Click **Google Map** from the **Quick Build** tab (Interactive Objects) and drag the insert cursor across your page to set the map size.

2. From the Google Map dialog, enter your post code (zip code) or address in the **Search for a location** field, then click **Search**. As Google's geolocator is being used, WebPlus will sense your locale, and display local addresses preferentially.

Adding markers

You can add an unlimited number of **markers** to your Google Map. Each marker can display further details on hover over and mouse click.

To add a marker:

1. From the Google Map dialog, click **Add**.

2. In the Google Map Marker dialog, click a chosen location using the $-\frac{1}{1}-$ cursor.

3. Enter a **Name** for the marker. This "tooltip" displays on **hover over** and could represent a company or site name.

4. Assign a **Click action** to the marker, i.e. what gets displayed on button click.

5. (Optional) Check **Open InfoWindow by default** for your label to display without the marker being clicked.

6. Click **OK**. The marker appears on the map preview in green (to indicate it is currently selected). Repeat the process for each additional marker you wish to add.

External / Managed Content

6

Inserting a blog

A blog acts as a personal journal on your web page that hosts your own published articles and offers an easy-to-use text editor. Articles can be commented on by visitors to the web page.

In WebPlus, blogs are actually **Smart Objects** (p. 164), a common term to indicate that they are intelligent server-sided objects hosted on the secure online service called **Serif Web Resources**. As a result, a pre-requisite to using blogs, like all Smart Objects, is that you have a valid Serif Web Resources account which you can create as you create your blog.

As a blog owner, you can manage the blog. Articles can be added, edited, or removed, while visitor's article comments can be deleted. Another feature is the ability to allow multiple authors to add articles to your blog (see WebPlus Help).

If you're on the move or working remotely, you can always monitor and update this managed content by using **Serif Web Resources**. A republish of your website is not necessary.

Inserting blogs

Blogs are like any object in WebPlus, in that you can easily insert one onto a chosen page.

To insert a blog (on the page):

1.   From the **Quick Build** tab (External / Managed Content category), click **Blog**.

2.   Drag the   cursor across your page to define the size of your blog region.

   If you don't have a Serif Web Resources account (or are logged out), you'll get the Serif Web Resources login dialog. To sign up, click **Create Account** under the **New User?** section.
   - or -
   If you're an existing user and are already logged in, you'll get an **Edit Blog** dialog.

3.   From the dialog, enter a **Name** for your blog. This is the blog title that appears at the top of the published blog.

4.   (Optional) Add a **Blog Description** to describe your blog's subject matter. Options are described in detail via the dialog's Help button.

5.   Click **Save**. The light blue region defines the blog area.

To edit your blog:

●   Double-click the blog.

Managing your blog

Managing your blog lets you add, edit, or delete articles, and even comments associated with articles. You can also select an **Editor group** for multi-author article publishing. For new articles (or when editing) you can create/edit your article in RTF, add tags, pick an article poster, allow trackbacks, and make comments.

To manage your blog:

- Select the blog and click 🔍 **Manage** from the context toolbar.

> For more management information and a description of each option, click the Help button in the blog's Smart Object dialog.

Inserting a forum

WebPlus lets you insert a Forum Smart object into your site, which can be structured into separate categories containing one or more subforums.

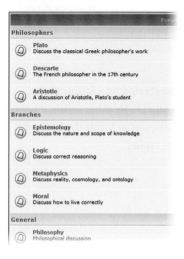

For example, you could create the categories Philosophers, Branches, and General, while the Philosophers category would include the subforums Plato, Descarte, and Artistotle.

Visitors can view the topics posted in a subforum, the number of replies/views, the topic author, and the last post. The selection of a topic lets the visitor post a reply or start a new unrelated topic.

Nottingham Philosophy Club ⚡FAQ 🔍Search 👥Memberlist ✏️Register 📶RSS
Philosophical Discussion

Philosophy
Moderators: None

Users browsing this forum: None

[📝 new topic]   Nottingham Philosophy Club Forum Index -> Philosophy   Mark all topics read

	Topics	Replies	Author	Views	Last Post
🔘	On being a community of thinkers	54	robin	107	Tue Jun 16, 2009 9:33 am beatingdrum →🔲
🔘	New Forum Features	0	abha	15	Wed May 06, 2009 12:05 pm abha →🔲
🔘	Philosophy-related events	10	abha	43	Sun Jun 22, 2008 7:08 pm abha →🔲
🔘	Appearance and Reality	1	Geoff	80	Mon Jun 16, 2008 11:50 am tom →🔲
🔘	Free will and punishment	42	tom	80	Fri Apr 11, 2008 10:27 am Geoff →🔲
🔘	socratic method	0	Geoff	132	Thu Apr 10, 2008 8:43 pm Geoff →🔲
🔘	Philosophy Blues (or reds)	27	Adrian	546	Fri Apr 04, 2008 10:13 am Adrian →🔲
🔘	New members	10	Adrian	70	Fri Apr 04, 2008 10:11 am Adrian →🔲
	Display topics from previous: All Topics ▾ Go				

[📝 new topic]   Nottingham Philosophy Club Forum Index -> Philosophy   All times are GMT

Page 1 of 1

Within a selected subforum, a topic can be created by a forum visitor which can be viewed and/or optionally replied to by other forum visitors (by posting a message in response). This discussion forms the basis of forum debate, creating a "thread" of visitor replies.

Forum features

- Create different **categories** (e.g., Philosophers) containing multiple **subforums** (Plato, Aristotle, Descartes, etc.).

- Establish **access control** for users and moderators.

- Set forum **privacy** as publicly readable or private.

- Apply a **theme** (style) to the whole forum.

- Create, edit, and assign **user ranks**.

- Set **user permissions**.

- **Manage** and **moderate** the forum without republishing.

> If you're on the move or working remotely, you can always monitor and update this managed content by using **Serif Web Resources**. A republish of your website is not necessary.

Inserting a forum

A forum can be added to the page like any other object, although you have the option to present the forum in a full-size window as an **offsite link** instead.

To insert a forum:

1. From the **Quick Build** tab (External/Managed Content category), click **Forum**.

2. Drag the ⊕ cursor across your page to define the size of your forum region.

If you don't have a Serif Web Resources account (or are logged out), you'll get the Serif Web Resources login dialog. To sign up, click **Create Account** under the **New User?** section.

- or -

If you're an existing user and are already logged in, you'll get an **Edit** dialog.

3. From the dialog, enter a **Name** for your forum. This is the forum title that appears at the top of the published forum.

4. Add a **Forum Description** to describe what the forum is for.

5. Click **Save**. The forum appears on your page.

> If you already have an Access Control smart object present in Serif Web Resources that you would like to use, this will be displayed in the **Access Control (Existing)** drop-down list for selection. Alternatively, you can just create a new Access Control smart object for the new forum by checking **Access Control (New)**.

> You can also create a forum by selecting **Smart Object** from the **Insert** menu.

To edit your forum:

• Double-click the forum.

> For more details about Serif Web Resources account control, see **Using Smart Objects** (p. 164).

Managing your forum

Up to now, you've just created a default forum—a single subforum within a single category. To edit category name, subforum name, and add more categories and/or subforums within those categories, WebPlus lets you manage the forum. You can also control forum privacy, moderation, theme, and user ranking (most posts).

To manage your forum:

• Select the forum and click **Manage** from the context toolbar.

• To explore the available options, scroll down and click **Help** at the bottom of the dialog.

Forum security

By default, your forum is created with the **Add new users on signup** feature enabled, which means you don't need to do anything except moderate forum content when needed. Forum contributors simply register and enter their own login details to post or reply to topics.

Technically, a forum uses a User List Smart object for access control, which is created along with your forum if you have the **Access Control (New)** option checked (see above).

Remember that a forum is a Smart Object itself! It is possible to use the **User List** Smart object to manage forum users in several ways:

• **Manually add users**. You can add a set of users for private forums rather than have new users sign up by themselves.

• **Ban/suspend users**. In a lively debating environment, there's often the need for some timely moderation to keep forum contributor's on-topic and adhering to "house" rules. You're able to ban or suspend users accordingly.

To manually add forum users:

1. Select **Smart Object** from the **Insert** menu.

2. From the Smart Objects library list, select the User List smart object of the same name as your forum.

3. Click **Manage**.

4. Use the **Users** and **Groups** tabs to manually add users, and the **Bans** tab to ban/suspend users.

5. Click **Exit**.

> Forums, by their nature, are complex objects. For more configuration details and a description of options, click the Help button in any Smart object dialog.

Inserting an RSS reader

WebPlus lets you include an RSS feed from another website on your own web page.

The addition of the RSS feed reader to your page automatically subscribes to the chosen RSS feed, which will keep feed content updated without editing and republishing your site.

To insert an RSS feed on your page:

1. Locate and copy an RSS Feed URL from a website to the clipboard by right-clicking the RSS symbol.

2. From the **Quick Build** tab (External/Managed Content category), select **RSS Reader**.

3. A place cursor is displayed. To set the size of the feed window, drag out a region and release the mouse button. Instead, for a window of default size, simply click the mouse.

4. In the dialog, paste the feed's URL into the **RSS Feed URL** field.

5. Click **OK**.

Social Media

7

Inserting a Facebook widget

Facebook widgets can be added to your page to stream various types of live feeds to display on your page or a Like button that allows users to share and promote your page via their Facebook pages.

A Facebook account is recommended to use these widgets. For more information about Facebook, visit **www.facebook.com**.

Inserting a Facebook widget

The widget is placed directly on the page, the same as any other object.

To insert a Facebook widget:

1. From the **Quick Build** tab (Social Media category), click
   Facebook Widget then click on the page to place.

2. In the dialog, from the **Type** drop-down list, select either **Activity Feed**, **Like Feed**, **Recommendations Feed**, or **Like Button**.

3.   In the **Preview** pane, check or uncheck **Update** to preview what your widget will look like on the page as you make changes.

4.   Customize the behaviour of your widget:

 •   **Use Current Site URL**
     Check to use the current URL of your site. Uncheck to enter a custom web address below. For Like Feed, enter the exact URL of a Facebook page.

 •   **Link Target** (Recommendations Feed only)
     Select **Blank** to open links in a new window, select **Parent** or **Top** to open links in the same window.

 •   **Verb to Display** (Like Button only)
     Select **Like** or **Recommend** as the word that appears on the button.

5.   (Optional) Customize the appearance of your widget using additional options (these differ according to Type).

6.   Click **OK**.

Editing a Facebook widget

Once added to the page, the Facebook widget can be edited at any time.

To edit a Facebook widget:

1.   Double-click the widget. The **Edit** dialog is displayed. The options available are the same as those available when the widget was created.

2.   Make your changes and click **OK**.

Inserting a Twitter widget

A Tweet or Follow button can be added to your page that interfaces directly with Twitter.

> 🐦 Follow @SerifSupport   950 followers
>
> 🐦 Tweet   195

⭐ A Twitter account is recommended to use these widgets. For more information about Twitter, visit **www.twitter.com**.

Twitter widget types

There are two types of widgets that can be added to a page to allow visitors to engage with site content in different ways.

Widget type	Features
Tweet Button	Allows visitors to share your website by tweeting your site content to their Twitter profile.
Follow Button	Allows visitors to follow your account on Twitter.

Inserting a Twitter widget

The widget is placed directly onto the page, the same as any other object.

To insert a Tweet Button:

1. From the **Quick Build** tab (Social Media category), click
    Twitter Widget then click on the page to place.

2. In the dialog, from the **Type** drop-down list, select **Tweet Button**.

3.   Customize the behaviour of your button:

- **Use Current Site URL**
  Check to use the current URL of your site. Uncheck to enter a custom web address in **URL To Tweet**.

- **Tweet Text**
  Enter Tweet Text. This text gets displayed in the Tweet field and is modifiable prior to Tweet submission.

- **Via**
  Enter the name of a Twitter account to add to the end of the tweet as a "via @<username>". It is recommended to enter your username in this field.

- **Recommend**
  Offers a recommended Twitter username that web visitors can follow. The recommendation appears after a Tweet has been submitted.

- **Hashtag**
  Enter a phrase as a hashtag (phrases cannot have spaces). Tweets will be searchable by that hashtag.

4.   (Optional) Customize the appearance of your widget using additional options (these differ according to Type).

5.   Click **OK**.

To insert a Follow Button:

1.   From the **Quick Build** tab (Social Media category), click **Twitter Widget** then click on the page to place.

2.   In the dialog, from the **Type** drop-down list, select **Follow Button**.

3.   In the Preview pane, check or uncheck **Update** to preview what your widget will look like on the page as you make changes.

4. In **User To Follow**, enter a Twitter username. Visitors will follow this account on Twitter when they click your button.

5. (Optional) Customize the appearance of your widget using additional options (these differ according to Type).

6. Click **OK**.

Editing a Twitter widget

Once added to the page, the Twitter widget can be edited at any time.

To edit a Twitter widget:

1. Select the widget already present on your page.

2. Double-click the widget. The Edit dialog is displayed. The options available are the same as those available when the widget was created.

3. Make your changes and click **OK**.

Inserting a Google +1 button

Promote your site by using a Google +1 button to let visitors recommend your site content to **Google+**. When visitors click your button they will be able to share your web page by posting on their live stream or the +1 tab on their Google+ profiles. The +1 tab displays all links a user recommends to the public. The Google +1 button can also display how many others have recommended your web page.

A Google+ account is recommended to use this button. To find out more about Google+, visit **plus.google.com**.

1.   From the **Quick Build** tab (Social Media category), click
     Google +1 Button then click on the page.

2.   From the dialog, in the Preview pane, check or uncheck **Update** to
     preview what your widget will look like on the page as you make
     changes.

3.   In the **Configuration** pane, check **+1 Current Page** to use the
     current URL of your site. Uncheck to enter a custom web address in
     Custom URL.

4.   (Optional) From the **Size** drop-down list, select a size for your
     widget.

5.   (Optional) From the **Annotation** drop-down list, select an
     annotation style.

6.   Click **OK**.

1.   Select the button already present on your page.

2.   Double-click the button. The **Edit** dialog is displayed. The options
     available are the same as those available when the button was
     created.

3.   Make your changes and click **OK**.

Inserting a social bookmarking button strip

If you add a strip containing a selection of social bookmarking buttons, your web visitors can share and promote your site via whichever social media or social news site is clicked. WebPlus lets you to create a strip with some of the most popular social websites including Facebook, Twitter, Reddit, Digg, etc.

Although not considered social media, the strip also lets visitors share your site's URL via email or simply print the current page.

Why not position your button strip on a master page? This will make the strip available across all pages that use that master page.

To insert a social bookmarking button strip:

1. From the **Quick Build** tab (Social Media category), click **Social Bookmarking Button Strip** then click anywhere on the page to place it.

2. From the dialog, select a website from the **Not Included In Strip** list and click **Add** to add that website's button to the strip. To remove a button from the strip, select a website from the **Included In Strip** list and click **Remove**.

3. (Optional) Click **Up** or **Down** to change the order icons appear on your strip.

4. Select a **Share** option: **Site** to share your entire site, or **Page** to share just the page.

5. Click **OK**.

To edit a social bookmarking button strip:

1. Select the button strip already present on your page.

2. Double-click the button strip. The **Edit** dialog is displayed. The options available are the same as those available when the button was created.

3. Make your changes and click **OK**.

Media

8

Inserting videos

WebPlus includes an optimized and highly-compatible video player from Flowplayer that lets you place individual videos and playlists directly on your page. You can use videos from your own computer, or stream videos that exist elsewhere online. The player is versatile with a customizable appearance that gives viewers access to all the playback controls they'd expect, including watching videos full-screen.

Supported video formats

The primary supported video format is MP4 (.mp4). For extended compatibility, Flowplayer can supplement MP4 video with WebM (.webm) and Ogg Video (.ogv) variants to use where MP4 is not supported. Flowplayer achieves excellent compatibility using the modern HTML5 standard to stream video without requiring a browser plug-in, but on older computer systems where HTML5 is not supported Flowplayer can fallback to using a Flash Player instead.

You can also stream Flash Video (.flv) in a Flash Player, but this option is increasingly unpopular as it is not widely supported by handheld devices.

Adding one or more videos to your page

Videos are inserted in a player straight on the page. You can include a single video, or add multiple videos to make your own playlist. Playlists allow you to show visitors a sequence of videos one after the other within one player.

To insert a single video or playlist:

1. From the **Quick Build** tab (Media category), click **Video Player**.

2. Position the ⊕◉ cursor where you want the video player to appear on the page, then simply click the mouse.

3. Choose the format for your video player:

- **Use HTML5 and MP4 video**
  HTML5 offers the **best compatibility** playback with no browser plug-in or media playing software required.
  - or -

- **Use Flash video**
  Choose the older Flash video player for Flash FLV video.

4. Add your video or videos to the player:

- **Add individual videos**
  - or -

- **Add all videos in a folder**
  - or -

- **Add videos from your Assets**
  - or -

- **Add a video that is already online**

5. (Optional) To remove a video from the playlist, check the box to the left of its thumbnail and click **Delete**.

6. (Optional) To adjust video order in a playlist, use the △ **Up** and ▽ **Down** buttons at the bottom of the dialog.

7. Click **OK**.

See WebPlus Help for further information about player and playlist configuration.

The video player will be inserted where you clicked on your page and by default will be sized to match the first video in your playlist. You can **configure the player** to adjust its size and appearance and also customize playlist control buttons.

To replace a video or edit the playlist

For an existing video player, you can go back to your video selection or playlist and edit it at any time.

To replace your video or edit the playlist:

1. Double-click the video object on your page.

2. Follow **Steps 4 to 8 above** to add videos, delete a video, reorder the playlist, or add WebM and Ogg videos to supplement MP4 files.

Resize and configure the video player

Customize the size and basic appearance of the video player while setting it up or at any time afterwards.

To customize a video player:

1. Double-click an existing video on your page and click the **Settings** tab.

2. Choose a clip or predefined dimensions from the **Size** list on the **General** tab to set the player size. It's recommended that your player is sized to match your video (or smaller) rather than choosing a player size larger than your clips.

3. Choose a **Skin** to set the player's basic appearance.

4. Pick **Colours** for your progress bar and other elements.

5. Replace the **Poster image**—the preview shown in the player before your video or playlist begins.

6. Choose the **Controls** that you would like viewers to be able to use.

7. Set optional player **Behaviour**.

8. Enable or disable player **Controls**, such as the mute button, volume slider, and 'get embed code' button for sharing videos on other sites.

9. (Optional) Click **Assets** to save these configuration settings to your Assets for future use, where they can simply be dragged and dropped onto a video object from the Asset tab to load your preferred settings.

You can customize the player even further if you have multiple videos in a playlist by choosing new **Playlist Buttons**.

Adding and customizing playlist control buttons

When you have more than one video in a playlist viewers can use buttons to select another video from the sequence, or skip to the previous/next video in the list. You can also customize these buttons using ready-made artwork and buttons of your own design. Please see WebPlus Help for more information about choosing and configuring playlist buttons.

Inserting YouTube videos

YouTube videos that are already published on the Internet can be included on your web page. YouTube videos themselves are not embedded in your site; instead, just the unique video ID is embedded as you place the YouTube video on your page.

To embed a single YouTube video:

1. Open the **www.youtube.com** website in your browser, and choose the YouTube video that you want to link to.

2. Copy the URL address for the video (or embed code). This contains an alphanumeric ID which uniquely identifies the video clip.

3. From the **Quick Build** tab (Media category), select 🔲 and click on your page.

4. In the dialog, ensure that Single Video is listed in the **Choose a video selection** drop down. Paste the video URL, ID, or embed code into the input box.

5. (Optional) To just play a snippet rather than the full video, specify start and end times (in seconds).

6. Click **OK** if you are happy to insert the video in a standard YouTube player.

To swap your YouTube video for another, double-click an existing YouTube video. From the dialog, paste a previously copied video URL into the input box. Consider embedding a **YouTube playlist** instead of a fixed choice of individual videos if you want to update video content on your site without using WebPlus.

See WebPlus Help for information about adding and creating YouTube playlists.

Inserting Vimeo videos

Vimeo videos that are already published on the Internet can be included on your web page. Videos themselves are not embedded in your site; instead, just the unique Vimeo video ID is embedded as you place the Vimeo video on your page.

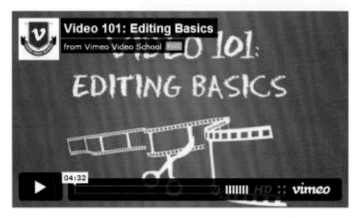

To embed a Vimeo video:

1. Open the **www.vimeo.com** website in your browser, and choose the Vimeo video that you want to link to.

2. Copy the URL address for the video (or its embed code). This contains an alphanumeric ID which uniquely identifies the video clip.

3. From the **Quick Build** tab (Media category), select [vimeo] and click on your page.

4. In the dialog, paste the video URL into the input box.

5. (Optional) Choose a custom colour for the player controls and any visible text to match or contrast with your site using the **Colour of Video Controls** selector.

6. (Optional) Check/Uncheck the boxes to enable/disable video options.

7. Click **OK**.

Inserting Flash SWF files

A Flash SWF file is a viewable movie, animation, or interactive feature using the Flash™ Player format. (Flash is a vector-based program designed to create and display small files on the web.) You can preview the Flash file and/or customize the effect. Once placed into your site, the animation will appear static, but they will spring to life once the site is previewed or has been exported and a visitor views your page in a web browser.

⚠ Please be aware that web browser support for Flash animations and movies is restricted to regular computers—most modern tablets and smartphones cannot display Flash content, so you should consider using an alternative format.

To insert a Flash file:

1. From the **Quick Build** tab's Media category, select ![Flash icon] **Flash** and then click on your page.

2. Select the Flash file to open (click **Browse** or **Browse Assets** then select your SWF file). Click **Export Options** to optionally define a different file name and/or file location. To keep the animation separate from the WebPlus file (using a link to the source file) uncheck **Embed Flash files in site**.

3. (Optional) In **Additional Files**, build up a library of files (e.g., images) that are used to make up your Flash movie. Think of it as a local library in which supporting files are easily at hand and easily referenced. Click the **Add File from Disk** or **Add File From Assets** button to navigate to then select files from your computer drive or stored within a custom Asset Pack.

4. (Optional) The **Display Options** tab controls how the Flash movie is presented on your WebPlus page. Experiment with the options for different looping, transparency, alignment, scaling, and quality options.

5. (Optional) In the **Flash Parameters** tab, click the **Add** (or **Edit**) button to add (or edit) parameters as name/value pairs.

6. (Optional) Apply standard object **Actions**, **ID / Anchor** options, or **CSS Properties** using the universal settings tabs.

7. Click **OK**.

To edit a Flash movie:

•   Double-click your Flash movie.

Forms

Inserting forms

Web-based forms allow information to be collected from visitors to your website in an efficient and modern manner.

Form data can be collected in a variety of ways—by email, to a local/remote script file, or via Serif Web Resources. See **Submission of forms** on p. 126.

Form Structure

The building blocks of a form comprise a mixture of text labels and form fields. A field can be for a button, edit box, date picker, text area, combo box, check box, radio button, file upload, or CAPTCHA object. A typical form, perhaps an email feedback form, is made up of a combination of some of these fields.

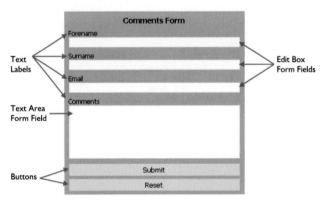

From the web visitor's perspective, information is typed into text boxes or selected from check boxes, radio buttons, or drop-down boxes. The information entered can be numeric, textual, or a mixture of both, depending on the type of field. The tab order by which fields are to be completed is configurable, as is validation of input data. (See WebPlus Help for more about tab order and validation).

Each field has its own set of properties relating to its appearance, its value(s), validation, or the action expected of the field.

A form's functionality only becomes active when your website is published (of course you can still preview your forms from within WebPlus, see **Previewing your site** on p. 153). When a web visitor enters data into, or selects a form option, the data will be sent back to a chosen destination when the form is submitted.

Creating forms

Two methods exist for creating forms:

- Using a **form template** from **Form Designer**, a purposely designed environment for creating and modifying forms. You can choose to keep the template as is or modify it to your requirements.

Form Templates are available for appointments, comments, and login. Other popular forms that could be created from scratch by the user include CV submission forms and canvassing forms.

- Using an on-page **blank form** and adding form fields from the **Quick Build** tab.

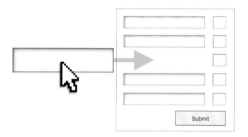

Creating forms (from a template)

The easiest way to create commonly used forms is to select one of the Form Designer's impressive range of form templates. These templates can be used without modification so they're almost ready to go—all you need to decide is where the submitted form data should be sent to. It's also easy to modify the template to your requirements by adding, deleting, or modifying individual fields.

To create a form using a template:

1. From the **Quick Build** tab, select ![icon] **Form** from the Forms category and click on the page.

2. From the **Form Designer**, ensure the **Templates** tab is selected, then select a form template from the tab pane (e.g., Login, Appointment, etc.). Use the right-hand preview window to review each template.

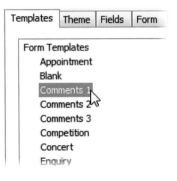

3. From the **Theme** tab, select a specific look for your form.

4. (Optional) From the **Fields** tab (Add Field), click additional field to add them to your form. Delete unwanted fields or rearrange fields using the buttons under the preview page.

5. From the **Forms** tab, set a **Form Name**, **Form Title**, and **Width** for the form (not form fields).

6. From the **Form Submission** tab, choose a destination for your form data by clicking a destination button for Serif Web Resources, email, or script file (local or remote) and a name to define the whole form. (See Submission of forms on p. 126).

7. Click **OK**.

> If you haven't set up form submission, you'll be prompted to return to the Form Designer (by clicking Cancel) and set up how a user's form data is to be submitted. If you click OK, it's assumed that you'll set up form submission later.

The form is added to your page.

Customizing template forms

If you've selected a template form you can customize it to your own requirement. Form fields can be modified, reordered, or removed. Additional form fields can also be added.

To modify a field:

1. From **Form Designer** (**Templates** tab), double-click a form field in the right-hand preview pane.

2. Edit the **Field Properties** in the **Fields** tab. Options differ depending on the type of form field selected.

3. Use the default internal **Name** for the field (to uniquely identify it) or edit it, and then modify the **Label** to accompany the form field (this is shown on-screen).

To reorder fields:

-   Select a form field in the preview window, then click **Move Up** or **Move Down**.

To remove a form field:

-   Select a form field, and click **Delete**.

To add additional fields:

-   Select the **Fields** tab and click the type of field you want to add.

> To add supporting text to your form (e.g., a competition question), you can click **Text Label** in the **Advanced** category.

For pre-populated combo boxes (such as Countries, UK Counties, US states, etc.), click **Assets** and select the **Load field from an Asset Pack** option from the flyout. The Asset Browser lets you select from the Combo Boxes category.

Creating forms (from scratch)

If you're looking for design freedom, WebPlus lets you create a blank
form directly on the page to which you can add form fields.

To create a blank form from scratch:

*   From the **Quick Build** tab, **Ctrl**-drag [icon] **Form** from the Forms
    category to the page.

The blank form, composed of a blank form area and a Submit button, is
added to the page. You can then add form fields to the form easily.

To add form fields to the form:

*   Click a form field, e.g. an Edit Box, on the **Quick Build** tab and then
    click in a form area to place the field.

Once form fields are positioned within the form, they are attached to it.
You can position the form and individual form fields using dynamic
guides, page guides or column/row guides like any other objects.

Forms as Assets

Some forms and form fields are assets, and as such belong to specific
asset packs. WebPlus lets you navigate from the Form Designer to your
Asset Browser and select an alternative form template (or form field) to
use.

You can also store any custom field or entire form to a custom asset
pack for future use. Fields can also be loaded from an Asset pack.

To access forms via the Asset Browser:

1. In **Form Designer** (**Templates** tab), click **Browse Assets**.

2. Select a form from the Asset Browser's **Page Content>Form Templates** category.

If you wish to store your own form field that you've modified from a template or created from scratch, it can be saved as an asset. See WebPlus Help.

Editing forms on the page

If you've created a form using a template it can be edited in Form Designer at any time. Forms from scratch can be edited on the page.

To edit a template-based form:

1. Double-click the form.

2. In the Form Designer, select a form field for editing or apply a different theme from the **Theme** tab.

On the page, the form will always remain locked to prevent accidental editing. If you want to have form design freedom you can unlock it.

To unlock a template form for editing:

*   From the Form context toolbar, select 🔗 **Unlock Form**.

> ⚠ Once you've unlocked your form, you'll gain design freedom, but won't be able to use the Form Designer again.

Unlocked forms and forms you create from scratch can be edited using normal object control in WebPlus. The form bounding box can be resized, pictures can be added to the form, and form fields can be ordered and rearranged. Form field properties can also be edited independently of Form Designer.

To edit form fields:

- Double-click the form field.

Submission of forms

All forms have one thing in common—they must be submitted to allow data to be collected. This is done by the website visitor using a dedicated **Submit** button form field when using **Form Designer** or when creating a form **from scratch**. The button needs to be present on the form.

Where is data sent?

After submission, form data can be sent to one of the following:

- **Serif Web Resources**; for transit of submitted form data to your email (via Serif), using CAPTCHA gateway security.

- an email address (of the web developer).

- a script file (stored locally or remotely); this could write text to a text file or into a server database.

These submission options can be set up within Form Designer, using the **Form Submission** tab.

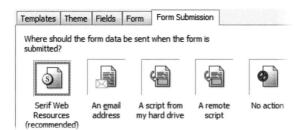

For option-specific settings, see WebPlus Help.

Text

10

Importing text from a file

Importing text from a word-processor file is a quick way to build up text content for your site (but you can also create a story using WritePlus). If you use your current word processor (such as Microsoft Word) to create the text files for your site, you can import any number of files into one site.

As well as the WritePlus format (.stt), a range of popular word processing and text formats can be imported, including:

ANSI text	.txt	Open Office text	.odt
Microsoft Word 2007/2010	.docx/.dotx	Rich Text Format	.rtf
Microsoft Word 2000/2003	.doc/.dot	Wordperfect	.wpd
MS Works	.wps	Write	.wri

For Microsoft Word formats created in any Windows operating system you don't need to have Microsoft Word installed locally. This means you can reuse third-party text content in WebPlus without the supporting application.

WebPlus will import text into a selected **text frame** or create a new text frame if one is not selected. See **Inserting text frames** on p. 33 for more information.

WebPlus will preserve the formatting of imported word-processor text. However, if you're using your word processor to create text specifically for WebPlus, you'll save time by typing as text only, and applying formatting later in WebPlus.

To import text into a new text frame:

1. Choose **Insert > Text File** from the **Text** menu.

2. From the **Insert Text File** dialog, select the format of the source file to be imported and locate the file itself.

3. Check the **Retain Format** box to retain the source file's formatting styles. Uncheck the box to discard this information. In either case, WebPlus will preserve basic character properties like italic, bold, and underline, and paragraph properties like alignment (left, centre, right, justified).

4. Click **Open**.

5. Drag out to place the text frame at your chosen dimensions.
    - or -

    Click on the page or pasteboard to create a new frame at a default size.

You can also import text directly into a text frame which already exists on the page.

To import text into an existing frame:

1. If using an existing empty text frame, select the frame. If inserting text into a populated text frame, click for an insertion point (or select a portion of text to be replaced).

2. Follow procedures 1-4 **above**.

The text will be imported into the selected text object. For text frames, the text may overflow your frame. To resolve this, see **Controlling overflowing frame text** on p. 34.

Using artistic text

Artistic text is standalone text you type directly onto a page. Especially useful for headlines, pull quotes, and other special-purpose text, it's easily formatted with the standard text tools.

HAC HABITASSE

To create artistic text:

1. Choose the **A** **Artistic Text Tool** from the **Drawing** toolbar.

2. Click anywhere on the page for an insertion point using a default point size, or drag to specify a particular size as shown here.

3. Set initial text properties (font, style, etc.) as needed before typing, using the Text context toolbar, **Text** menu, or right-click (choose **Text Format**>).

4. Type directly on the page to create the artistic text.

Once you've created an artistic text object, you can select, move, resize, delete, and copy it just as you would with a text frame. Solid colours, gradient/bitmap fills and transparency can all be applied.

To resize or reproportion an artistic text object:

- Drag the object's corner handles to resize it while maintaining the object's proportions.

- To resize freely, hold down the **Shift** key while dragging.

To edit artistic text:

- Drag to select a range of text, creating a blue selection.

You can also double-click to select a word.

Now you can type new text, apply character and paragraph formatting, edit the text in WritePlus, apply proofing options, and so on.

Editing text on the page

You can use the Pointer Tool to edit **frame text**, **table text**, or **artistic text** directly. On the page, you can select and enter text, set paragraph indents and tab stops, change text properties, apply text styles, and use Find and Replace. For editing longer stories, and for more advanced options, choose WritePlus (**Edit Story** from the **Text** menu).

Selecting and entering text

The selection of frame text, artistic text, and table text follows the conventions of the most up-to-date word-processing tools. The selection area is shaded in semi-transparent blue for clear editing.

Nulla vestibulum eleifend
nulla. Suspendisse potenti.
Aliquam turpis nisi, venenatis
non, accumsan nec, imperdiet
laoreet, lacus.

Double-, triple-, or quadruple-click selects a word, paragraph or all text, respectively. You can also make use of the **Ctrl**-click or drag for selection of non-adjacent words, and the **Shift** key for ranges of text.

To edit text on the page:

1. Select the **Pointer Tool**, then click (or drag) in the text object. A standard insertion point appears at the click position (see below).
    - or -
    Select a single word, paragraph or portion of text.

2. Type to insert new text or overwrite selected text, respectively.

    Nulla vestibulum eleifend
    nulla. Suspendisse potenti.
    Aliquam turpis nisi, venenatis
    non, accumsan nec, imperdiet
    laoreet, lacus.

To start a new paragraph:

*   Press **Enter**.

To start a new line within the same paragraph (using a "line break" or "soft return"):

*   Press **Shift+Enter**.

To switch between insert mode and overwrite mode:

● Press the **Insert** key.

Copying, pasting and moving text

You can easily copy and paste text using standard commands; drag and drop of text is also supported.

> If you don't place an insertion point, the text can be pasted into a new text frame directly.

Assets for Creativity

11

Using assets

An **asset** is a general term for any object or page element that can be added to your page to enhance its appearance, increase efficiency, or personalize your design. Assets range from graphics, **pictures**, picture frames, **buttons**, **sliders/panels**, various settings, to more complex page content and entire **pages**.

To use assets, WebPlus provides the **Assets tab**, powered by both an **Asset Browser** (p. 139) and **Asset Manager**. The former browses your assets, the latter lets you create and manage custom Asset Packs.

> **Theme Layout** design templates come complete with their own built-in assets, all themed to the site's design. When you start from a theme layout the **Assets** tab will be populated with associated assets automatically!

Using the Assets tab

The **Assets** tab is a powerful design resource that exclusively hosts your browsed assets, ready for adding to your web page from the following categories.

- **My Designs**: Stores custom assets dragged from the page.

- **Graphics**: Contains professional clipart from Asset Packs.

- **Pictures**: Added pictures from your hard disk (or from Asset Pack, if containing pictures).

- **Page Content**: Contains navigation bars, buttons, sliders, panels, picture frames, forms/form fields as well as text frames and shapes.

- **Pages**: Complete ready-to-go pages from Asset Packs.

- **Settings**: Contains settings for page backgrounds, CSS properties, button/ separator designs, form themes, and video player settings.

- **Resource Files**: Contains supporting script files (JavaScript, CGI, etc.), favourites icons, PDF files, and any other files that you may need to include in your site.

The tab also lets you save your own page objects for reuse globally or for use just in your site (by dragging to the My Designs category or dragging to another tab's category respectively). Settings, rather than actual objects, can be saved exclusively to the tab's Settings category.

See **Storing custom assets and asset settings** (see p. 145).

Browsing for assets

Although initially empty, the tab can be populated with pre-designed assets by using an Asset Browser.

The Asset Browser

The Asset Browser lets you browse by asset category and Asset Pack (Pack Files), as well as search (by tag) for assets. Once displayed, the asset can be selected for inclusion in the **Assets** tab.

The Asset Manager

Use the **Asset Manager** to create your own Asset Packs by using assets from other Asset Packs and/or by importing pictures, graphics, or PagePlus pack files. You can tag assets and then save or export your custom asset pack. See WebPlus Help

Asset browsing

The **Asset Browser** offers a whole range of professional ready-to-go designs, called assets, that you can use directly in your site. These designs are provided in categorized pack files (also known as Asset Packs), installed with WebPlus.

There are two ways to browse assets before adding assets to your workspace—by category or by pack file.

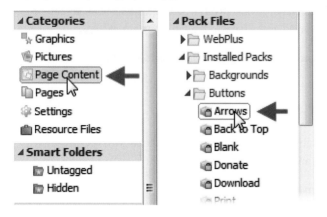

You can also use the search controls at the top-right of the dialog to narrow your search, or to find a specific assets in the pack files.

To browse assets (by category):

1. From the **Assets** tab, click  **Browse**.

2. In the Asset Browser, select an asset category from the Categories section.

For example, for Graphics, you'll see available graphics appear in sub-categories (e.g., Boxes, Flags, etc.) in the main pane.

3. Scroll through the sub-categories to browse and select additional assets.

To browse assets (by Pack File):

1. From the **Assets** tab, click [ ] **Browse**.

2. In the **Asset Browser**, on the left-hand side of the dialog, select a pack file category (e.g., Backgrounds) or asset pack name from the **Pack Files** section. You may need to click the ▶ right arrow to expand a category for the latter. The pack file(s) will appear in the main pane.

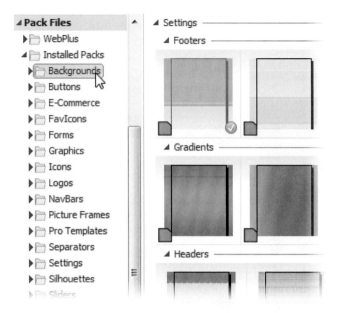

3. Scroll through to browse the assets included in each pack file. To make browsing easier, you can expand and collapse the categories or pack files to hide or reveal the assets.

Searching for assets

The search facility filters assets based on preset and custom tags applied to all of the pack files shown in the **Asset Browser**.

To apply a search filter:

- For a simple tag search, type the word or letter you want to search for in the **Search** text box, situated at the top right of the dialog. This is useful for retrieving assets with custom tags attached.

If your search results are being restricted to the currently highlighted category, Smart folder, Smart tag, or pack file, you can click the appropriate section header to remove this restriction.

Filtering assets

Filtering means that you can restrict the amount of assets on display.

- For **category** and/or **pack file filtering**, select a category or pack file (or multiple instances using **Ctrl**-click). You can also search for category and pack file combinations. For example, **Ctrl**-clicking the Graphics category and then a Theme Layout gives you just graphics from that theme layout.

- For **Smart tag filtering**, select a tag name from the **Smart Tags** section (scroll down the left-hand pane). Smart tags let you filter assets logically by subject matter using a hierarchical and alphabetic tag structure. For example, if you select the "Wildlife & Nature" tag you'll see all assets tagged with that tag; if you want Animal-only assets, you could select "Animal", nested under that Occasions tag.

> ◢ ▢ Wildlife & Nature
>   ▢ Animal,
>   ▢ Birds
>   ▢ Cats

- For **tag-specific filtering**, select a tag name from the **Tags** section of the Asset Browser (below the Smart tags section). Use **Ctrl**-click to manually select multiple tags.

Adding assets to your Assets tab

To add a specific asset:

● Select the **category** or **pack file** in the Asset Browser, and then simply click the asset. A check mark shows on the thumbnail.

To add all assets:

● Click **Add All** ⊘ from the upper-right corner of each Asset Pack's thumbnail gallery. Check marks will show on all thumbnails.

With either method, asset(s) will be available to you from the **Assets** tab when you close the Asset Browser.

> Any asset stored in your **Assets** tab (but not added to the page) will be available to you the next time you open your site. Assets can be made globally available by **pinning** in the relevant tab category. Custom designs can also be made global by dragging page objects to the tab's My Designs category.

Adding assets to your page

To add an asset to the page:

● Click and drag a thumbnail in the category onto the page.

Storing custom assets and asset settings

WebPlus lets you create and store custom assets from objects on the page; the settings of an object (its colour) can also be saved. This allows the assets to be used again either in your current WebPlus site or globally in any site in the future.

Objects and their settings can be stored, as custom assets, within Assets tab categories as follows:

Assets tab category	Store object as custom Asset	Store object settings as asset
My Designs (from drawn vector shapes, line art, and artistic/frame text); stores assets for global use	Y	N
Graphics (from drawn vector shapes, line art, and artistic/frame text); stores assets for site only	Y	N
Pictures* (from adjusted or cutout pictures)	Y	N
Page Content* (navigation bars, buttons, forms)	Y	Y
Page Content* (text frames, adjusted pictures, picture frames, sliders, panels)	Y	N
Pages*	Y	N
Settings* (backgrounds, form themes, navigation bars, buttons, CSS properties, video player, e-commerce item options, e-commerce price breaks, e-commerce shipping information)	N	Y

> ✦ * When you close your site, any assets you've created in these categories will need to be saved. You'll be prompted to save a custom Asset Pack specific to the site.

Objects and settings are added to the Assets tab by dragging from the page, then dragging back onto your page where (and when) you want it.

> ✦ Pages are added to the Assets tab from within the tab category.

Storing to My Designs

If you're keen on storing your own objects for **global** use, the **Assets** tab's **My Designs** category is ideal—the stored assets will always be available in any new site you create.

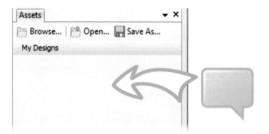

When you first install WebPlus, the My Designs gallery will be empty, ready for objects to be added to it.

To store an object in My Designs:

● Drag the object from the page and drop it onto the **Assets** tab's My Designs category.

If you drag an object to any other category, then it will only be available to the current site.

Storing Pages

Any page already present in your site can be stored in the **Assets** tab (Pages category).

To store a page:

1. From the **Assets** tab's Pages category, click **Add**.

2. From the dialog, check a page (or master page).

3. Click **OK**. The page appears in the Pages category.

Storing asset settings

Instead of storing an object, it's possible to store just an object's settings for reuse at a later date. As an example, a custom button's design could be saved, rather than the button itself.

Like storing objects, settings can be stored by drag and drop of the object, but to the Settings category only. A pop-up dialog lets you choose the type of settings needing to be saved.

Pinning categories and individual assets

Individual assets and entire categories within the **Assets** tab can be made available for all sites (i.e., globally) if they are pinned.

To pin and unpin assets:

- To pin all the assets in a category, click **Pin All** on the category header.

  - or -

  To pin an individual asset, click the icon on the individual asset.

- To unpin all the assets in a category, click **Unpin All** on the category header.

  - or -

  To unpin an individual asset, click the icon on the individual asset.

Previewing and Publishing

12

Using Site Checker

In advance of publishing, the **Site Checker** searches your website for common layout problems relating to site navigation, text formatting, forms, and E-Commerce, and reports detected problems. A wide variety of commonly encountered problems can be located but typical problems include:

- Duplicate object HTML IDs.

- Invalid Anchors or Hyperlinks.

- Web Forms: No Submit button or form objects have the same name.

- W3C validation failure warnings.

- Large JPG images exported as PNG.

- Overlapping, rotated, or cropped text.

- Non-WebSafe fonts.

A full list of checks performed is shown via the Site Checker's **Filter Site Problems** button.

If problems are found, the Site Checker reports each problem in a problem list along with options to fix or hints to resolve the issue.

If you're not concerned with certain problem types or you would like to postpone resolution to a later date you can use **problem filtering**. (See WebPlus Help.)

1. Click **Site Manager** on the Default context toolbar, then select **Site Checker**.

2. (Optional) Select whether to view problems for **All Pages** or a specific page from the **Page** drop-down list.

3. In the **Type** drop-down menu, choose to view **All Site Problems** or selectively choose to view problems relating to:

    - **Site Navigation**

    - **Text Formatting**

    - **Form and E-commerce**

4. Click the **Start** button to begin the search for problems, which will be listed automatically.

By default, issues are listed according to Page order, but the list contents can be reordered by clicking column headers.

Click on an individual problem entry in the list to view any suggested Primary or Secondary fix (shown in lower text box).

1. Check the **Page** check box at the top left of the problem list to select all pages and problems.

2. Click the **Fix All** cell at the bottom right of the list. The row will show multiple problems selected (e.g. 6/6 Selected).

3. From the **Apply Multiple Fix** dialog, click a button to apply either a **Primary fix** (most recommended) or **Secondary fix**. Problems that can be resolved automatically will be fixed and removed from the problem list once the appropriate button is clicked. However, some fixes may require modification of settings via additional dialogs.

4. Click **Close** to exit Site Manager.

To fix selected problems manually:

1. Double-click the **Fix** or **Hint** cell at the end of a specific problem list entry.

2. From the dialog, follow the displayed instructions as recommended, using the **Display** button to jump to the problem object (e.g., form) or page.

3. If the **Edit** button isn't greyed out, it can be clicked to launch the appropriate dialog needed to remedy the problem. If greyed, just follow the instructions for resolution.

4. Click **Close** to exit.

> If you want to temporarily (or permanently) ignore specific problems, click **Ignore Problems Of This Type**. See Filtering site problems in WebPlus Help.

Previewing your site

Previewing your site in a web browser is an essential step before **publishing it to the web**. It's the only way you can see just how your site will appear to a visitor. You can **preview** a page or site at any time, either within WebPlus (using an internal window based on the Internet Explorer browser) or separately using any browser installed on your system.

To preview your site:

1. Click the down arrow on the  **Preview site** button on the **Standard** toolbar.

2. Select an option from the submenu:

    •   **Preview in Window** (shortcut **Alt+P**) opens the site in a new internal WebPlus window.

    •   Choose **Preview in** to use an external browser. The names will reflect which browsers are currently installed, e.g. the entry may read "Preview in Internet Explorer." The site is exported to a temporary folder with the current page appearing in the specified browser; use any navigation bar to navigate to other site pages.

WebPlus allows you to view estimated download time for each page of your site, and provides information such as the number of files on each page and the total size of the files. This is carried out via the **Standard** toolbar's **Preview site** flyout.

Publishing to the web (using WebPlus.net)

Serif provides competitively priced web hosting that offers various levels of service to suit your individual requirements.

You can upload your site to WebPlus.net (Serif Web Hosting) so it's viewable by the whole world! You can specify that all web pages are published or, if updating your site, only pages changed since the last "publish."

To publish your site to WebPlus.net:

1.  Click the down arrow on the **Publish site** button on the **Standard** toolbar and click **Publish to Web**.

2. From the **Publish To Web: Get Hosting** dialog, click **Activate Now**.

Publish To Web: Get Hosting

Before you publish your website, you need a web hosting account.

Set up Serif WebPlus.net hosting & a domain name.	**Use existing hosting & domain name.**	**Publish your website later.**
WebPlus.net hosting is the easiest and most convenient way to get your website live online – we'll even give you 30 days of free hosting.	If you already have your own WebPlus.net or third party hosting, just put the details into WebPlus to get your website online.	If you don't want to setup your hosting yet, you can do it later.
It only takes a minute to set up and no technical expertise is required.		
Activate Now	Add Details	Cancel

3. Follow the set up procedure within your default Internet browser. You'll be provided with a hosting page which contains FTP details you'll need to manually transfer.

4. In WebPlus's **Account Details** dialog, transfer hosting details from your hosting setup page and paste them into the equivalent fields, e.g.

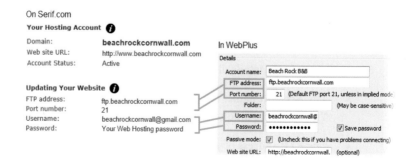

On Serif.com

Your Hosting Account

Domain:	**beachrockcornwall.com**
Web site URL:	http://www.beachrockcornwall.com
Account Status:	Active

Updating Your Website

FTP address:	ftp.beachrockcornwall.com
Port number:	21
Username:	beachrockcornwall@gmail.com
Password:	Your Web Hosting password

In WebPlus

Details

Account name:	Beach Rock B&B
FTP address:	ftp.beachrockcornwall.com
Port number:	21 (Default FTP port 21, unless in implied mode
Folder:	(May be case-sensitive)
Username:	beachrockcornwall@
Password:	●●●●●●●●●●● ☑ Save password

Passive mode: ☑ (Uncheck this if you have problems connecting)

Web site URL: http://beachrockcornwall. (optional)

5.   Click **OK** to close Account Details.

6.   In the **Upload to server** dialog, click the **Test** button to test your FTP Account. If the test is successful a dialog will display stating that a connection has been established.

7.   Click **Update Account**.

The **Publish To Web** dialog can then be used to upload your website.

Publishing to the web (using a third-party host)

Publishing to the web using a third-party host involves uploading your site to a web host provider you've arranged independently of Serif.

To publish your site to the web:

1.   Click the down arrow on the **Publish site** button on the **Standard** toolbar and click **Publish to Web**.

> If you've not set up FTP account information, you'll be prompted to add FTP details via a pop-up dialog.
>
> If you've set up at least one account, the **Publish to Web** dialog appears with the last used account name shown in the drop-down list and its settings in subsequent boxes.

2.   From the **Publish To Web: Get Hosting** dialog, click **Add Details**.

3.   In the **Account Details** dialog, enter:

   •   The **Account name**. This can be any name of your choice. You'll use it to uniquely identify this account in WebPlus.

   •   The **FTP address** of your web space—this is a specific URL that will be provided by your web host.

- **Port number**: Unless directed by your provider, you can leave this set at "21."

- Leave the **Folder** box blank unless directed by your provider, or if you want to publish to a subfolder of your root directory.

- You'll also need a **Username** and **Password** as pre-assigned by the provider.

- Check **Save password** to record the password on your computer, if you don't want to re-enter it with each upload.

- **Passive mode**: Leave checked unless you are experiencing FTP connection problems.

  If you are certain that the FTP details are correct, unchecking **Passive mode** might fix the problem. ISPs and web hosts can operate passive or active FTP modes of operation, so it is worth checking this with them.

- **Web site URL**: Set your site's URL. This allows you to view the web site from a dialog after FTP upload.

- Click **OK** to close Account Details.

4. Back in the **Upload to server** dialog, click the **Test** button to test your FTP Account.

5. Click **Update Account**.

Quick Publish

Quick Publish allows you to quickly upload and view the currently displayed page—useful for live verification of individual pages.

To configure Quick Publish:

1.   Click the **Publish site** flyout on the **Standard** toolbar and then click **Quick Publish Configuration**.

2.   In the dialog:

   • Enter the details of, or select from the drop-down list, the URL of the site you want to publish to.

   • Select the browser to view your page once it has been published.

   • Select the FTP account you want to use from the drop-down list. To update account settings, or add a new account, click **Manage Accounts**.

3.   Click **OK**.

To Quick Publish to Web:

   •   Click the **Publish site** flyout on the **Standard** toolbar and then click **Quick Publish to Web**.
   The **Uploading files** dialog briefly appears before your page is displayed in your chosen browser.

Advanced Content

13

Understanding e-commerce

E-commerce entails the buying and selling of goods on the Internet. Any site that supports this kind of e-commerce activity will typically make use of a shopping cart system and a payment processing system. A shopping cart is a virtual basket (think of a supermarket basket) which stores your chosen items and is used in conjunction with a payment processing system (taking the place of the supermarket's checkout).

WebPlus allows you to choose one of several specially chosen shopping cart providers and, secondly, it allows you to connect to the shopping cart provider via a form or link on the WebPlus page. Forms allow for buying options such as size and quantity (below) to be set, along with button choices, currency control, description fields, and more.

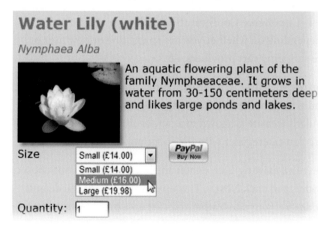

E-commerce forms also let you calculate tax rates, shipping, bulk items, etc.

Links offer simple one-click purchasing without buying options.

The features are provider-specific and as a result, vary widely.

Configuring your shopping cart provider

A number of different shopping cart providers can be configured within WebPlus. These are the most commonly used and some, like PayPal®, you may have come across directly as an eBay® customer. The configuration process directs you to the provider's own site from where you can sign-up as a registered user.

> Use the provider's website to find out more about unique shopping cart features.

To set up a shopping cart provider:

1. From the **Quick Build** tab (E-commerce), click [icon] **E-Commerce** then click on the page to place.

2. From the **E-Commerce Configuration** dialog, you have two options depending on whether you are an existing or new user of one of the shopping cart providers, i.e.

   - If you're a new user, select a shopping cart provider by enabling its radio button, then click the **Sign Up Now** button. The provider's website is shown in a new browser window from where you can register with the shopping cart provider.

   - If you're an existing user, enable the button next to your chosen provider, and click **Next>**. This option simply sets the default provider for your site (rather than set up a provider account).

3. The dialog is provider-specific and may show different options. As an example, choosing PayPal lets you define (via dialog) an email address to receive payments, cart handling charge, and use a "Sandbox" test tool for trying out your shopping cart before going live. Click **Next>**.

   For Sandbox testing, click the **Find Out More** button to setup a separate Sandbox login in addition to your "live" PayPal login.

4. (Optional; PayPal only) In the next dialog, check **Use the PayPal Minicart** to display a pop-up cart (as an overlay) that appears as products are added to the cart (the cart is subsequently minimized to the top-right of your browser window while items remain in your cart before checking out).

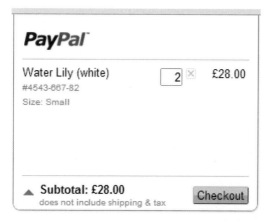

You can also configure, via the dialog, the minicart position in your browser window and edit or delete the default text displayed in the Minicart.

5. Click the **Finish** button to complete shopping cart configuration.

Once you've configured the shopping cart, you'll need to Insert an e-commerce object such as a form or link that is specific to your provider. This can be done immediately after shopping cart setup or at any time via **Insert>E-Commerce Object**.

See WebPlus Help for more details.

Using Smart objects

For managed content, WebPlus uses server-sided **Smart objects** which store gathered web visitor data on Serif's own secure server space called **Serif Web Resources**. You can manage your smart objects directly from within WebPlus, or independently, and at any time, via **www.serifwebresources.com** once your site is published and live.

Let's look at each Smart object you'll find in Serif Web Resources and what you can do with them.

Accommodation Booker

Host the online booking of guest house, motel, and bed & breakfast rooms, with pricing options for different date periods and days of the week.

Active Viewers

Use to show how many people are currently viewing the web page.

Blog

A blog acts as a personal journal on your web page which hosts your own published articles in an easy-to-use text editor. Articles can be commented on by visitors to the web page.

You can also drag a blog onto the page by using the **Quick Build** tab.

Content Management System (CMS)

Lets the web developer add content to web pages remotely without accessing and publishing via WebPlus. Content is article-based where articles can be categorized, created, edited, deleted and arranged into categories. Site visitors can comment on and rate any article.

Forum

Add a thread-based discussion forum to your site, split into multiple categories and subcategories. You can also drag a forum onto the page by using the **Quick Build** tab.

Hit Counter

A straightforward count of the number of hits on the current page (reset as needed). Different styles can be adopted.

News

Add a news window onto your page.

Poll

Set up an online poll to canvass web visitor's opinions.

Resource Booker

Host the online booking of meeting rooms, rehearsal rooms, theatre tickets, and more. Book by the hour or by the day, as recurring bookings, and with pricing options for different age groups.

Shout Box

Acts as an interactive chat window similar to Windows Messenger. Let your web visitors chat amongst themselves.

User List

The User List Smart object operates in two modes (each mode selectable via a pop-up dialog):

- **Mailing List mode**: Have website visitors sign up to newsletters, party confirmations, information request, and many more. Lists can be controlled manually or by self-subscription. Email addresses can be imported as a delimited text file (CSV) or export to a range of formats.

- **Access Control mode**: Control accessibility to pages, forums, blogs, and CMS by using user groups. See **Access Control** on p. 171 for more details.

  o   Enable CAPTCHA anti-spam protection during user registration.

  o   Create user groups (with optional user sign-up, auto-login, and connection to Smart objects).

  o   Add, remove, suspend, or ban users.

As Smart Objects are stored in Serif Web Resources, you can use Help buttons accompanying each Smart Object (as you create and manage them) for more detailed information.

For security reasons, the objects are only available via a **Serif Web Resources** login accessible from within WebPlus. If you don't have a valid username and password you must create a Serif Web Resources account first.

- If your email address is already known to Serif (maybe you've just registered or have registered previously) you'll be asked for a limited number of questions to complete account registration.

- If you're new to Serif and unregistered you'll have to complete full security as required. Full instructions are provided on login screens.

To create a Serif Web Resources account:

1.   From the **Insert** menu, select **Smart Object**.

2.   In the login dialog, click the **Create Account** link under the login boxes.

3. In the next dialog, enter your current email address, screen name, and a password twice. You'll need to review and agree to Serif's terms and conditions of use (via a check box).

4. Click the **Signup** button.

5. An additional dialog, will ask for personal details, plus a few check boxes if you would like to receive the Serif Community newsletter, Serif offers, and/or other third-party offers.

6. A confirmation email will be sent to your email address. Click the link in the email and you're ready to login to Serif Web Resources (via **Insert>Smart Object**).

To clear Account details:

- Go to **Tools>Options** and click **Clear Account Details** shown from the **Options>General** menu option. This will clear the stored login details for Serif Web Resources so that automatic login will no longer work. Details will need to be entered next time so be sure you've remembered your password.

To access Web Resources:

1. From the **Insert** menu, select **Smart Object**.

2. At the login prompt enter your username and your password. Check **Remember account details** to access Web Resources directly in future (bypassing the login screen).

3. Click the **Login** button. The Smart Objects dialog is displayed.

> Once created, you can check your account details from the Smart Objects dialog by clicking the **My Account** button.

To log out of Serif Web Resources:

- From the Smart Objects dialog, click **Log out**.

Creating Smart objects

Smart objects can be created via Serif Web Resources, by adding to a Smart Object library (the library lets you manage and edit each object). Objects can then be added to the web page immediately or at a later date.

Some Smart objects such as **forums**, **blogs**, and news windows can be dragged onto the page from the Quick Build tab.

Some Smart objects have interdependencies between each other. An example is the Forum Smart Object which when created, creates a User List smart object for access control as well.

To add an object to the library:

1. From the **Smart Objects** dialog, click **New**.

2. In the **Create Smart Object** dialog, use the scroll bar to navigate the list, then select a Smart object.

3. (Optional) For your Smart object to operate in a language other than English, select from the **Language** drop-down list.

4. Select **OK**. Depending on the type of object selected, a different Create dialog will be displayed for the Smart object.

5. From the dialog:

   - Enter your own Name for the object.

   - (Optional) Select a Profile if created previously.

   - (Optional) Add a Filter Offsite string (access to the object will be restricted to the domain entered and will prevent the URL from being copied).

   - (Optional) Change the object's titling, colours (for body, text and border), and border thickness if appropriate.

6. Click **Create**.

The named object will be shown in a list in the My Smart Objects Library left-hand pane.

To add a Smart object to your web page:

1. From the Smart Objects dialog, select the chosen object from the left-hand pane and click the **Insert** button.

2. To insert the object at a default size, position the ✛▇ cursor, then simply click the mouse.

   - or -

   Drag the cursor across the page to size the Smart object.

The Smart object will automatically preview on the page so you'll get a good feel for how your published Smart object will look.

Editing Smart objects

Once an object is created it can be edited either in the My Smart Object Library or directly on the page. Typically, you might want to alter the appearance of the object from its original settings, maybe change a Poll question, or reset a Hit Counter back to zero.

Editing an object only affects the object itself and does not alter any collected data.

The dialog options for editing and creating a Smart object are identical.

To edit a Smart object in your library:

- From the **Smart Objects** dialog, click the **Edit** button at the bottom of the My Smart Objects Library pane.

To edit a Smart object on your page:

- Double-click the object to reveal the object's **Edit** dialog.

Managing Smart objects

While editing Smart objects affects how the object operates, managing Smart objects can be used to manage the object's "gathered" data when the web page is published. Some Smart objects such as Hit Counters don't need to be managed as they just increment on each web visit (you can reset the counters though). However, other more complex Smart objects (e.g., Forums, Blogs, Accommodation Booker, Resource Booker, User List, Poll, and Shout Box) store collected visitor data such as article comments, email addresses, poll results, and a chat messaging log. For **Blog** and **User List** smart objects creating and managing articles or users, respectively, is a fundamental part of the management process.

To manage a Smart object from your library:

- From the Smart Objects dialog, click **Manage** at the bottom of the dialog. The management options differ for each Smart object type.

To manage Smart objects directly over the Internet:

- Login to **www.serifwebresources.com** to control all your Smart objects independently of your WebPlus site. Use your usual Web Resources login as before.

> For more management information and a description of each option, click the Help button in any Smart object dialog.

> The CMS Smart object can only be managed via **www.serifwebresources.com**.

Access control

Access control applies security to your site, either to restrict access to specific pages or to control user access to forums, blogs and CMS.

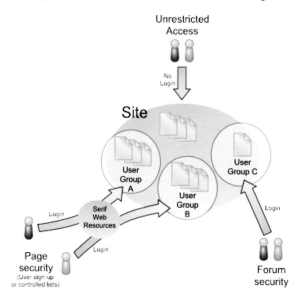

- **For page security**: lets you login to a password-protected page(s) or via an on-the-page login box. As an example, a personal Photo Gallery page can be made "private" but still be shared with a selected group of users (under password control). The login details are stored in a user group associated with the page which contains a list of authorized users; the users are added manually by the web manager of the site or new users can self-register via sign up.

- **For Smart object security**: provides access control for **forums**, **blogs**, and **CMS**.

  - Forums: for management of users and group moderation.

  - Blogs: for adding/removing articles via an Editors group.

  - CMS: for managing articles in your CMS.

Access control is possible via **Serif Web Resources** by using a **User List** Smart object (see p. 164), which can be created to manage user groups and users, and how users sign in.

CSS properties

In addition to styling attributes that you apply graphically in the main WebPlus workspace, like fill colour, outline etc., you can apply some additional **CSS properties** to objects. CSS properties are stored efficiently as code rather than being created as part of your graphics, and are applied dynamically by visitors' web browsers.

> CSS properties cannot be applied to all objects, but where it is supported can be applied in addition to regular graphical attributes, so you may need to check both kinds of styling if you want to reformat an object.

CSS properties allow you to specify a **border** with options for spacing (padding) and corner styles, an outline (simple outer border), a **background image**, and **visibility** (object transparency).

To apply or edit CSS style attributes:

- From the Properties toolbar, click 🗹 **Edit CSS Properties**.
  - or -

  Double-click on an object, then from the dialog, select the **CSS Properties** tab.

- 🗹 If an object already has CSS Properties applied to it, you can edit them by clicking the **Edit CSS Properties** button at the bottom-right of the selected object.

- Apply settings in each tab to control the browser-based styling options and object behaviours, clicking **Help** in any tab to see more detailed advice. Click **OK** when finished.

> Click the **Assets** button to save your settings for future use, or to load previously-saved settings.

Animated marquees

Animated marquees are a way to add horizontally scrolling text (e.g. news ticker), perhaps for an attention-grabbing headline or catch phrase.

You can choose the background colour, enter from one to three lines of text, define text properties (choose from any installed font), scroll direction, speed and alignment for each line. If you like, you can define any link destination type for the marquee (see **Adding hyperlinks** on p. 67).

Animated marquees appear as static graphics on the WebPlus page. They will animate when **previewed** or viewed in a web browser.

To create an animated marquee:

1. Choose **Interactive Object** from the **Insert** menu and select **Animated Marquee** from the submenu.

2. Select the number of lines of text, and format each line using the controls in the **Animated Marquee** tab.

3. (Optional) Use the **ID/Anchor** tab to edit the object's automatically-generated HTML ID or configure an **anchor**.

4. (Optional) Add browser-based styling options to the object, such as a border or background, using the **CSS Properties** tab.

5. Click **OK**.

6. Position your cursor, then click on the page to add your animated marquee at a default size.
   - or -

   Drag out a region on your page to create and size your marquee to specific dimensions.

To edit an animated marquee:

• Double-click the marquee. The **Insert Animated Marquee** dialog displays again with the current settings in place.

Additional Information

Contacting Serif

Help with your Product

On the web	
Com**m**unity**Plus**	**community.serif.com** Get answers and ask questions in the Serif community! Type 'WebPlus X7' to filter WebPlus only articles.
Serif Support	**www.serif.com/support** For Serif Account and Customer Service information.

Additional Serif information

On the web	
Serif website	**www.serif.com**
Main office	
Address	The Software Centre, PO Box 2000 Nottingham, NG11 7GW, UK
Phone	(0115) 914 2000
Phone (Registration)	(0800) 376 1989 +44 800 376 1989 800-794-6876 (US, Canada)
Phone (Sales)	(0800) 376 7070 +44 800 376 7070 800-489-6703 (US, Canada)
Customer Service	0845 345 6770 800-489-6720 (US, Canada)
Fax	(0115) 914 2020

Credits

This User Guide, and the software described in it, is furnished under an end user License Agreement, which is included with the product. The agreement specifies the permitted and prohibited uses.

Trademarks

Serif is a registered trademark of Serif (Europe) Ltd.

WebPlus is a registered trademark of Serif (Europe) Ltd.

All Serif product names are trademarks of Serif (Europe) Ltd.

Microsoft, Windows, and the Windows logo are registered trademarks of Microsoft Corporation. All other trademarks acknowledged.

Windows Vista and the Windows Vista Start button are trademarks or registered trademarks of Microsoft Corporation in the United States and/or other countries.

Google+ social service, Google Analytics web analytics service, and Google AdSense advertising service are trademarks of Google Inc.

Copyrights

Index

15